YOUR BRAIN ON SILICON

# TREO Fan Book

Jeff Ishaq

Printed in the United States of America.
Published by O'Reilly Media, Inc.
1005 Gravenstein Highway North, Sebastopol, CA 95472.

*Treo Fan Book*
Your Brain on Silicon
by Jeff Ishaq

O'Reilly books may be purchased for educational, business, or sales promotional use. Online editions are also available for most titles (*safari.oreilly.com*). For more information, contact our corporate/institutional sales department: 800-998-9938 or *corporate@oreilly.com*.

**Print History**
November 2004: First Edition.



ISBN: 0-596-00816-3

[W]

Editor:
Brian Jepson

Photographer:
Brian Jepson

Production Editor:
Darren Kelly

Art Director:
Michele Wetherbee

Cover & Interior Designer:
Aufuldish & Warinner
*www.aufwar.com*

Illustrators:
Robert Romano
Jessamyn Read

Copyeditor:
Nancy Reinhardt

Indexer:
Julie Hawks

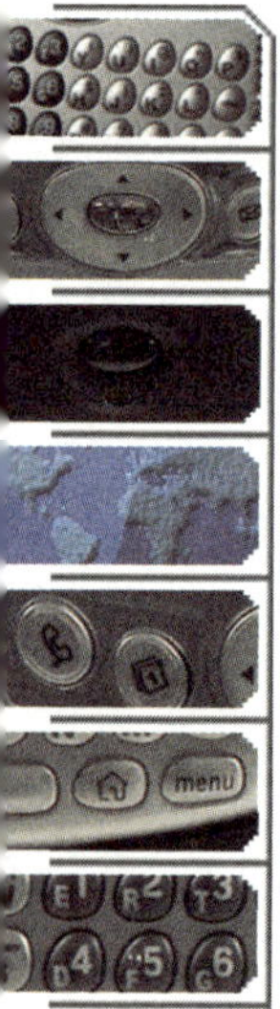



# Contents

Contents

# Preface

# The Treo Fan Book

Your Treo is a smartphone, a slippery phrase which denotes a cell phone that is powerful enough to have many features found on a desktop computer. For example, most smartphones feature email and web browsing, games, and the ability to run thousands of aftermarket applications—a *smart* phone.

The Treo allows you to place and receive calls just like any cell phone you've ever used, and it also happens to run the most popular handheld operating system on the planet: Palm OS. This means that, in addition to the built-in calendar, contact list, to-do list, and memo pad, you have quick access to tens of thousands of applications. These applications come in all categories, such as organizational and reference, games, office productivity, Internet tools, and phone enhancements, and I cover the very best in Chapter 6. As a seasoned Palm OS software developer, I can attest to the attractiveness of the OS, and to the booming software market. But Palm OS isn't the only game in town.

You may have seen other smartphones out there when you shopped for the Treo, and each smartphone runs a particular OS. Sure, there's lots of variation in hardware: some will have keyboards, and some are more like traditional cell phones with just a number pad and a cluster of navigation buttons; some will have touch screens, and some will not. But the look and feel, or usability, of the smartphone is deeply rooted in the OS that it runs. It is not my goal to cover all the smartphone hardware and OS choices on the market here. I assume you've done your homework, and even if you haven't—perhaps you impulse-bought a Treo, or received it as a gift—you still get an A+! You have picked *the very best* smartphone on the market. Really. There's something magical about the simplicity of the Palm OS, sometimes called The Zen of Palm, that promotes usability over everything else. It's impossible to find someone who doesn't love his Treo. *The Treo Fan Book* looks at how the Treo fits into your life and describes all the wonderful things you can accomplish with it, must-have accessories, and killer applications.

---

Having too many features is a bad thing. For more information on how The Zen of Palm keeps things usable, see *http://www.palmos.com/dev/support/docs/zenofpalm/ZenTOC.html*.

---

# Smartphones Versus Cell Phones

The most important feature that a smartphone holds over a cell phone is the ability to run tens of thousands of software applications—limitless expandability. These applications are typically downloaded over the Internet and very easily installed. They are usually freeware, or inexpensive shareware whose cost is truly commensurate with functionality. These are simple, cheap applications: you're probably not going to use Photoshop on your smartphone. But you never know what applications lay around the corner, and this unlimited potential for expandability is what is so cool about smartphones.

Buying a cell phone with a fixed set of applications and games is *so* 1990s. I believe that in the coming years, hundreds of millions of cell phone users will flock to smartphones for their expandability and, perhaps more so, for their convenient Internet access.

# Different Treos

Which Treo do you have? You may see a few different models of the Treo smartphone in use, and the following pages explain the differences between them. Cellular carriers will brand the Treo that works on their network accordingly, so don't be surprised to see other Treos in different colors than your own. Also, though the older Treo models are slower, and slightly larger, they still have a very loyal user base! Here are the Treos you will see in use today.

## Treo 270

The Treo 270 showed up in stores in May of 2002 and supports GSM networks, such as those operated by AT&T, Cingular, and T-Mobile. One feature that sticks out is its flip-top lid, which gave it great geek appeal. Flip the lid up to answer an incoming call, and then experience the satisfaction of hanging up by flipping your phone shut; with most modern phones, the action of physically hanging up a phone has atrophied into a mere button-press. Another cool feature that isn't quite as evident from the picture is fast (at the time it came out) Internet connectivity: the Treo 270 became one of the first phones that could surf *any* real-world web site, not just a handful of special phone-friendly sites, by using a GPRS data plan. The full keypad is well-received by anyone who has ever tried to compose an email or send a text message with a number pad, and a jog dial on the side of the phone allows for quick scrolling in lists and the like without whipping out the stylus. By pushing the jog dial in, the user can commit a selection.

Cingular's Treo 270 for GSM networks was the start of something very cool!

## Treo 300

In August of 2002, the Treo 300 was introduced, which despite the "better" version number, is essentially a light gray version of the 270. The difference between these two models is in the internal radio: the Treo 270 is designed to work on GSM networks, and the Treo 300 is designed to work with CDMA networks, such as Sprint.

## Treo 600

Sprint and HandSpring (now palmOne, Inc.) announced the Treo 600 on October 14, 2003, for use on CDMA networks. The GSM model came out soon thereafter. Unlike the Treo 270 and 300, the Treo 600 doesn't use a different model number to indicate the supported network technology; there is simply a GSM version of the Treo 600 that is light gray, and a CDMA version of the Treo 600 that is charcoal black.

These successors to the Treo 270 and 300 ditch the flip-top lid in favor of the "candy bar" phone style; its keyboard is slimmed down, sporting domed buttons for easier typing. The 270 and 300's jog dial is replaced by the five-way navigation pad, which integrates very closely with the operating system for intuitive and effortless screen navigation. The hardware and operating system have matured very nicely, with a fast CPU, a digital signal processor that can decode MP3 audio in the background, and Palm OS version 5.2.1.

This Treo 600 appears to have been attacked by a Be-Dazzler; in fact, it is encrusted with Swarovski crystals, and is owned by 17-time Grammy award-winning country singer Alison Krauss. Ok, you probably won't see this one among the general population, but it's still pretty cool.

The most expensive Treo 600 on the planet.

## Treo 650

The Treo 650 was announced in October of 2004. Its functionality and software are almost identical to the Treo 600, sporting mostly cosmetic improvements plus a few new features. The most significant feature is its gorgeous screen, which is extremely crisp, with twice the resolution (320 x 320 pixels) of the Treo 600. The battery life has been improved slightly, and the processor is considerably faster than the 600's, which is most beneficial for faster web browsing. Although the Treo 650 does not include the much-hoped-for one-megapixel camera, its VGA-quality camera is an improvement.

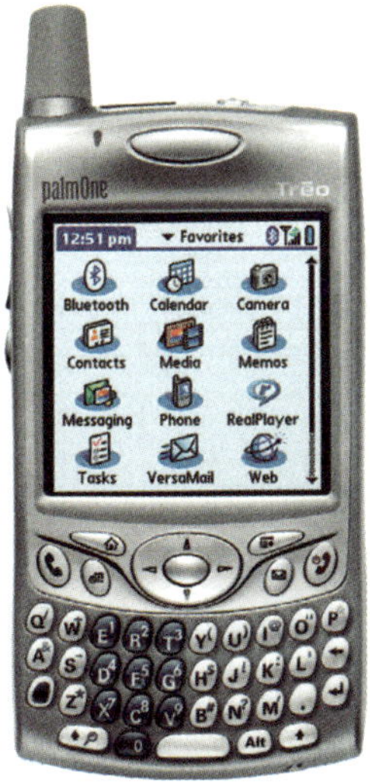


The Treo 650 can connect wirelessly to Bluetooth devices, such as headsets, keyboards, speakerphones, other handheld devices, and computers (for HotSync). The GSM version of the Treo 650 also supports EDGE (Enhanced Data rates for Global Evolution), a fast wireless data service offered by GSM providers such as Cingular. Many GSM customers can finally obtain data speed comparable to what Sprint and Verizon offer in the Treo 600.

# Where Are the Apps?

If you are eager to see what kind of applications you can run on your Treo, browse a few of the most popular online sites to check out the latest offerings. If your Treo has data service, you can certainly use it to browse these sites, but when it comes to browsing all the offerings you'll find there, it's usually more pleasant to do so from your desktop computer.

- Handango: *http://www.handango.com*
- PalmGear: *http://www.palmgear.com*

Most Palm OS software is either completely free, or comes in a trial version which typically costs $5 or $10 to unlock. Many people are surprised to discover that Palm OS software is very inexpensive! If you value the software in terms of its feature set, you will realize that you usually pay a small sum for a small set of features. Palm OS applications are simple in nature, so their feature set, and thus the price, don't become unwieldy as they can on other operating systems.

While browsing for applications, keep in mind that some Palm OS applications will state that they explicitly support one particular Palm OS device, such as the Treo 600. However, most of the Palm OS applications you see will run just fine on your Treo device—whether or not they explicitly state they support it. Such applications simply might not take advantage of some of the unique features of that device, such as a high-resolution display, or a 5-way navigation pad. If you're not sure whether an application will work on your Treo, download the trial version if one is available to try before you buy.

# 1

# Getting Familiar with Your Treo

# Why the Treo is Truly a *Smart* Phone

I've already covered what makes a smartphone. Here, I talk about what features make a phone smart. The Treo has two big features that make it just about the smartest phone you've ever used. The first is the seamless integration of the 5-way navigation pad into Palm OS applications, and the second is how the Treo keeps its data synchronized with your desktop computer.

## Smart Feature #1: The 5-way Navigation Pad

It doesn't take long to get used to the 5-way navigation pad, which exhibits the kind of intuitive product design that makes the Treo such a slick smartphone. There are five discrete functions of this pad Ⓐ: move up, move down, move left, move right, and activate (press center).

Henceforth, I'll refer to it simply as the navigation pad. You can use the navigation pad to move through user interface objects, such as buttons, lists, and editable fields. A blue box called the *focus ring* is drawn around the object that currently has the focus—that is, the attention of the operating system—and pushing the center button, which I'll call Center, in turn *activates* Ⓑ the object inside the focus ring.

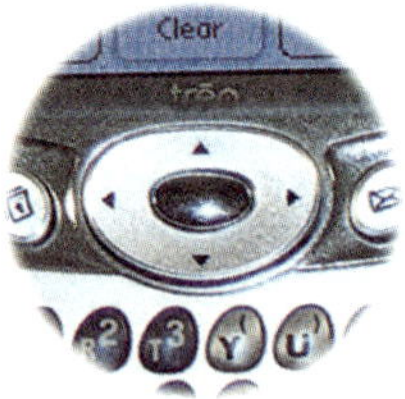


Ⓐ The Treo's 5-way navigation pad. Center is the fifth "way."

Ⓑ The focus ring indicates the OK button will be activated when you press Center.

The navigation pad permits you single-handedly to perform such tasks as selecting and activating one button among many, or scrolling through a list and selecting a particular item. When designing the layout of the Treo 600 device and the user's interaction with the operating system, HandSpring (now palmOne, Inc.) was very conscious of this single-handed usage model. I think it was designed very intuitively, and you'll see that after you get accustomed to the navigation pad, it becomes indispensable.

---

> It may seem trivial, but it really is painful for me to switch between using my Treo and using my older Palm OS organizers that don't have the navigation pad, because I have to dig out the stylus or poke at the screen with my finger.

---

The navigation pad is, for the most part, intuitive, but there are three behaviors that are better explained here instead of you figuring them out over time. Try them out once; chances are good you'll never forget them, and then we can move on. I've listed them in order of usefulness:

1. If you have activated a list (including a pop-up list), you can press the navigation pad to the left or right to deactivate the list and move the focus ring to the next thing on the screen. Doing this will preserve the list's original selection, even if you have highlighted something else.
2. The focus ring does not cycle. So if you have the focus ring around the top item on the screen, and you push up on the navigation pad, the focus ring will *not* shift to the bottom item.

3. The action of Center depends on the object in the focus ring. For simple things such as buttons and checkboxes, Center will "tap" that object. For more complex objects, such as text boxes and lists, Center will *activate* the object; while *activated,* the navigation pad will interact with that object, rather than move the focus ring. So, if you were to activate a list of items, you could work with it in three ways: you can scroll the items by pressing up or down; you can select an item by pressing Center; or, you can leave the list by pressing right or left to activate some other item.

If you have activated an editable field, pushing the navigation pad up/down/left/right will move the cursor position around the text of the field accordingly. If you attempt to navigate out of the bounds of the text—pressing up while on the topmost line of text, for example—the field will become deactivated, and the focus ring will move to the next thing on the screen. As a shortcut for this, hold down the Option key while pushing a direction on the navigation pad: the text field will be deactivated, and the focus ring will move in the direction you've pressed.

> The Treo 270's and 300's scroll wheel functions like a 3-way navigation pad: up, down, and center.

After you get used to the navigation pad, it will seem downright difficult to use any handheld organizer without one! The navigation pad allows you to perform most tasks single-handedly, without having to use one hand to hold the device and another to tap on buttons. Much like a scroll wheel makes mousing more efficient and more intuitive on desktop computers, the Treo's navigation pad is truly a quantum leap in the usability of Palm OS devices.

## Smart Feature #2: Effortless Desktop Synchronization

The second reason the Treo 600 is such a smart phone is its synchronization capability. This capability eliminates the tedious task of keeping your phone's data up to date with your desktop or laptop computer's data, and vice versa. If you've ever manually copied a phone number from your Mac OS X Address Book or your Outlook contact list into your phone (or vice versa), this is a feature you'll really appreciate. The Treo effortlessly keeps your contacts, appointments, to-do list items, and memos in perfect synchronization with your computer. If you have modified a contact on your Treo, and over on your computer you had to bump an appointment ahead a few hours in Outlook or iCal, one synchronization will propagate the changes between your Treo and your computer automatically.

palmOne's official phrase for the synchronization of data between your Treo and a desktop computer is *HotSync.* After you install the Palm Desktop software that comes with your Treo, HotSyncing is just a matter of connecting your Treo to your computer and invoking the HotSync by pressing the button on the HotSync cable.

In addition to keeping your contacts, calendar, notes, and to-do items in sync, many aftermarket Palm OS applications take advantage of the HotSync mechanism. One of the best examples of this is Cutting Edge Software Inc.'s *QuickOffice* suite, which I cover in Chapter 6. With QuickOffice, you can modify Microsoft Office documents on your computer *or* on your Treo. When you HotSync, the changes are automatically synchronized between the documents on your computer and your Treo.

Mac users will want to check out iSync, a slick solution from Apple that works with HotSync to provide more flexibility. iSync will keep your Treo synchronized with your Mac OS X address book, iCal, and to-do items, just as HotSync does. But with iSync, you can also control synchronization of your iPod or iPod Mini, as well as many models of mobile phones. You can also use your .Mac account to keep several Macs in sync with each other and access your data through ***http://www.mac.com***.

# Connecting for a HotSync

These days, you're no longer tethered to your desktop by a cable: you can HotSync in a variety of ways.

- There's the traditional USB or serial HotSync cable, which comes with your Treo, and simply plugs in to your computer and then to the bottom of your Treo. There are some super cool alternatives to the stock HotSync cable and charger—I cover those in Chapter 3.
- You can also use a cradle, which you have to order separately from palmOne, Inc. This is the same thing as the cable, except the cradle serves to hold the Treo at a convenient angle for hands-free viewing and use.
- For the road warrior, don't bother with the extra cable, but do keep a charger handy. If your laptop has an infrared (IR) port, you can perform an IR HotSync with no cables required! With a Bluetooth-enabled Treo and a laptop, you can do the same thing, but much faster.
- If you purchased an Internet plan from your Treo's service provider, and your desktop has a public IP address on the Internet, you can perform a network HotSync to your desktop from anywhere in the world, provided you're someplace where your Treo can connect to your service provider.

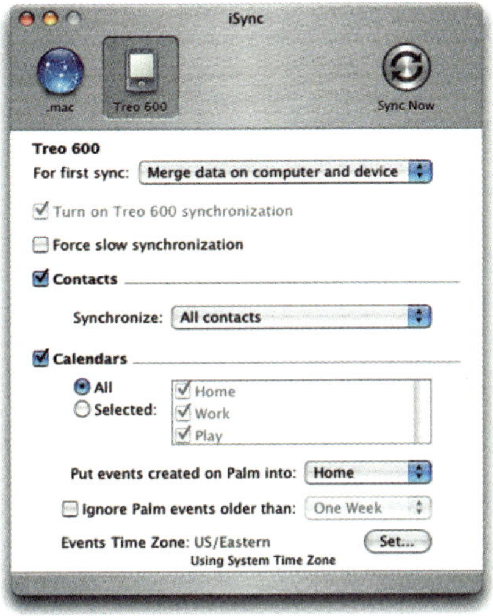


Apple's iSync provides a one-stop synchronization shop! These are the typical settings you'll use for the first-time synchronization to your Treo.

To use iSync, you must have first installed and configured the Palm Desktop software from the CD that came with your Treo. Then, download and install the iSync Palm Conduit from *http://www.apple.com/isync*.

Treo Fan Book

# A Quick Tour of the Hardware

When I first pulled my new Treo out of the box, there were so many buttons that I didn't quite know how to hold on to it. The thrill of a new toy! Here's a selective look at the device's more interesting hardware bits, to get you started without having to open up the dreaded manual.

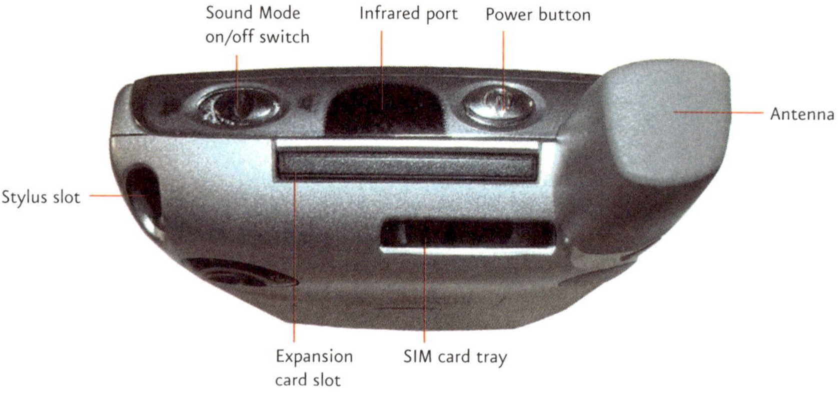


Looking at the Treo from the top, there are a few things to mention. From left to right, this figure shows: the stylus slot; the sound mode on/off switch; the infrared port on top; the expansion card slot in the middle and the SIM card tray (only on GSM phones) on the bottom; the power button; and the antenna.

## Sound Mode On/Off Switch

This switches between two sound modes that you can configure in the Sound section of the Preferences application. By default, Sound Mode Off will have no ring tone, but will vibrate instead.

## Expansion Slot

You can buy SecureDigital (SD) or MultiMediaCard (MMC) media that can hold up to an astonishing 1 GB of data. That's a lot of photos and MP3s!

## Power Button

Right, you know how a power button works, but it has additional functionality in that it toggles Wireless Mode. I go over this in Chapter 2.

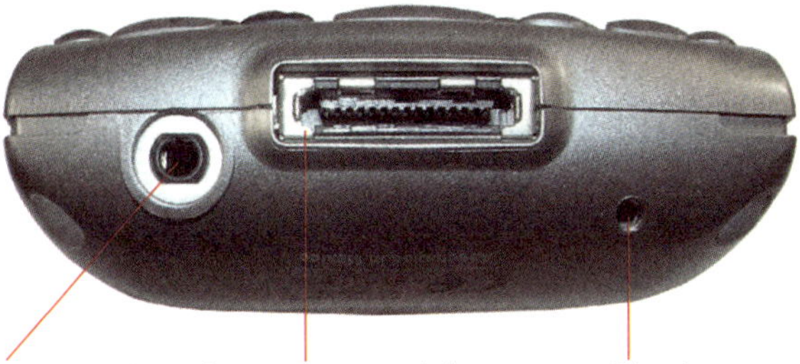


On the bottom, from left to right: the external headset jack, the HotSync and charger port, and the microphone. There's not much to say here, but I do cover some nifty aftermarket headsets in Chapter 5, and HotSync cables in Chapter 3.

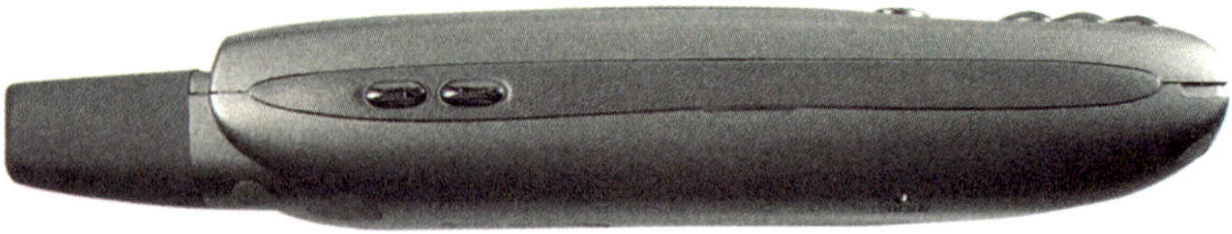

On the side, the only items of interest are the volume buttons. When you're on a call, the volume buttons will let you make your caller louder or quieter. When you're not on a call, the buttons change the ringer volume.

Ⓐ The Option Key lives to the left of the Z key

The picture of the keyboard shows a lot of stuff! The top row contains four shortcut buttons, as well as our good friend the 5-way navigation pad, which I already covered. If you launch the Preferences application, and then navigate to the Buttons section, you can reassign what the four shortcut buttons do. Here, each button can have two actions associated with it: one action that happens when the button is pushed, and one action that happens when the Option key (the key to the left of the Z key Ⓐ is held down while the button is pushed. The rightmost button is noteworthy because it powers the device on and off, exactly like the power button on top does. Why this redundancy? I don't know, so I suggest you remap this button to launch your favorite application!

The keypad block has the alphabet, backspace, space, and return keys. There are a few extra keys to note:

Home Key
: Remember this key! No matter what you're doing, this key will bring you into your Launcher so you can switch to another application. If you press it multiple times, it will cycle through the various application categories (All, Main, System, and so forth).

Menu Key
: If you are in an application that has menus available (which isn't always the case), this key will drop the menus down. A shortcut to get to the menu is to tap on the title bar, but because there isn't always a title bar, you sometimes need this button.

Alt Key
: This key lets you type in alternate forms of a character, useful for foreign languages. For example, to type in an *é:*

  a) Type the letter *e*.

  b) Push the *Alt* key.

  c) Select *é* from the pop-up list.

Preface
Getting Familiar with Your Treo
Using the Treo as a Phone
Staying Organized with Your Treo
Using the Internet on Your Treo
Amazing Treo Extras
Other Useful Stuff
Treo Fan Book

## Option and Shift Keys

You probably noticed that most alphabet keys have a second letter printed slightly above the primary letter. To get to this letter, you need to turn on Option mode first, by pressing the Option key. There are some nuances to both the Shift and Option keys that you need to know about. First, the mode of these two keys is always displayed on the bottom-right corner of the screen, as shown in the following table. Also:

### Delay

If you press and release either the Shift or the Option key, it remains active for three seconds or until you hit another key. This is useful if you don't have both hands free and you are unable to hold down Shift or Option and press another key at the same time.

### Lock

You can lock both the Shift and Option keys. The former is useful for yelling in all caps, and the latter is useful for entering in numbers. The lock is engaged by pressing the Shift or the Option key twice.

**Option and Shift Key Modes**

| Indicator | Mode |
|---|---|
| | Option mode engaged. This means the Option key is being pressed and held; or if it has been pressed and released, Option mode will disengage in three seconds, or after another key is pressed. |
| | Option mode lock. Until you disengage Option mode by pressing the Option key again, everything you type will be in Option mode. |
| | Shift mode engaged. This shows that the Shift key is being held and pressed; or if it has been pressed and released, Shift mode will disengage in three seconds or after another key is pressed. |
| | Shift mode lock. Until you disengage Shift mode by pressing the Shift key again, everything you type will be in Shift mode. |

Looking at the back you will find: the camera, two mysterious rubber plugs, the speaker, and the reset hole.

## Camera

Sprint offers a camera-less Treo 600, for those who work in secure environments where such devices are not allowed.

## Mysterious Rubber Plugs

The topmost and smallest rubber plug covers up a screw that attaches the built-in antenna to the device. The larger plug is for plugging in an aftermarket antenna to boost your signal strength. Such antennae are quickly going out of style as cellular coverage becomes ubiquitous, but for some people, the signal boost can make all the difference in the world.

## Speaker

This is actually the second speaker—it plays sound independently of the earpiece speaker on the other side.

## Reset Hole

Should your device crash or lock up, this is how you reset it. I cover these scenarios in Chapter 6. If you unscrew the tip of the stylus, the other side is the reset tool, though old school Palm users will insist on using a bent-open paperclip for this.

That's pretty much it for the hardware. Next, I will move on to the internals of the device: Palm OS.

# Getting Around in Palm OS

The Treo 600 ships with Palm OS version 5. If you have used other palmOne products, such as the Zire or Tungsten devices, things will pretty much look the same, because most of these products also run Palm OS 5. If you used a Treo 270/300 in the past, you were working with Palm OS 3, which has gone through considerable internal changes; however, aside from 5-way navigation, expansion card support (I cover this in Chapter 5), and a *huge* speed boost, you aren't likely to notice any functional differences between Palm OS versions 3 and 5. Regardless of whether or not you've used Palm OS, there are a few fundamental rules to keep in mind when working with the Treo:

1. Only one application can run at a time. In other words, the application you are looking at is the only game in town. This takes some getting used to coming from Windows, Mac OS, or Pocket PC environments, which allow you to have many windows open at once.
2. If you are on a phone call, you are still able to switch around to other applications as much as you'd like without dropping the call. So don't be afraid to look up an appointment while on a phone call, or even play Tetris. Having a headset, or using speakerphone mode, makes this a lot easier to do.
3. The Home screen, with all your applications' icons on it, is officially called the *Palm Launcher.* Palm Launcher is just another application, and you can always switch to it by pushing the Home button to the right of the spacebar. There are many aftermarket replacements for the Palm Launcher application; most notably, Zlauncher and Launcher X. I talk about Launcher replacements in Chapter 6.

4. Well-behaved Palm applications *expect* that you will switch out of them and into another application on a whim. For this reason, you don't have to concern yourself with the paradigm of "save your data before you exit," which is popular on desktop computers. Need to switch to the calendar in the middle of a memo, or make a phone call while halfway done with an email? Go right ahead! Memo Pad or Mail will be waiting for you when you return, right where you left off.
5. The Power button really just turns off the *screen*, and nothing more. When you turn the screen back on again, you'll be right where you left off, and no data is lost.

## Summary

These are the fundamental concepts you need to become savvy with the Palm operating system. The fact that they span a small number of pages is testament to the intuitiveness of the Palm OS, and to the usability of the Treo device. When you take your Treo out to send an email, to reschedule a meeting, or to place a phone call, you are not hindered by the device's physical layout, or by its operating system. In the computer industry, this is called good usability, and I am convinced this is the reason why the Treo 600 has been so well-received by savvy consumers.

Now please, play around with the device. Launch an application, fiddle around in it, hit the Home button, and launch another one. Try to use the 5-way navigation pad to get around, enter some text, and try doing a HotSync to your desktop. Next up, I'll talk about the expertise you need to use the Treo phone like a pro.

# 2

# Using the Treo as a Phone

In addition to running the most popular handheld operating system in the world, your Treo 600 is also a cell phone with more features than you could imagine. Out of the box, you are able to place and receive calls, manage call-waiting and join multiple callers into a conference call, set up call forwarding, and even turn on speakerphone mode. After you get accustomed to these conveniences, you can go online and explore the world of add-on freeware (or inexpensive shareware), written specifically for the Treo, which expands it in amazing ways. For example, CallFilter is an application that selectively filters callers to voicemail or to a landline, according to a schedule you define. There are hundreds of features you can add on to your phone simply by downloading and installing applications from the Internet. The choices can be overwhelming, but I tour the most useful ones in Chapter 6. Right now, I focus on the simpler aspects of the Treo 600 phone.

# Placing and Receiving Calls Like a Pro

It's pretty simple to place and receive normal phone calls on your Treo, as you would expect. But the Treo is much more than just a phone, and what follows are a few topics to give you a deeper understanding (and appreciation) of just how much *more* it can be.

## Wireless Mode

The last time you were on an airplane, you were asked to turn off your cellular phone before takeoff. The Treo provides a way to turn the cellular radio on and off, which it calls the *wireless mode*. When wireless mode is off, the cellular radio is off, and you are not able to place or receive phone calls, check your voicemail, or use the Treo's wireless Internet capability (if your service plan even provides it). However, you are still free to use your Treo as a normal Palm OS organizer and run applications, compose offline emails, and so on.

To toggle the wireless mode of your phone:

1. Make sure your Treo is on.
2. Push and hold the power button for a few seconds.
3. A carrier-specific splash screen will appear for a few seconds, followed by a tone (unless you have the phone in silent mode).
4. A short delay ensues while the cellular radio powers up or shuts down.

## Dialing

The Phone application is just another Palm OS application, just like Calendar or City Time. There are a few ways to launch the phone application.

1. By tapping on the Phone button

2. By selecting the Phone application in the Launcher

3. By answering an incoming phone call

After you are in the Phone application, you can simply dial a phone number and then tap the Dial button to place a call.

When dialing, you are free to use either the hard number keys on the keyboard, or tap the buttons on the screen.

For dialing when you are unable to look at the phone, there's a small plastic nub on the 5 key. It may seem a little daunting at first to dial on such a little keypad without looking at it, but it's really quite easy to get the hang of. Close your eyes and try dialing a number just by visualizing a phone pad, and using the plastic nub to keep your finger from going astray. It's not as hard as it first seems, and when you really need it, it's sure a nice skill to have.

I talk a little more about working with Contacts in the next chapter, but it isn't rocket science, so I assume you already have entered some contacts in your Contacts list (if not, try adding some right now and come back here when you are done). To dial a contact from your Contacts list, simply press down on the 5-way navigation pad to bring up the Contacts application.

I'm embarrassed to admit that the tip I'm about to give you took me about three months to discover—I actually had to read the manual—so take note! Here's how to locate a name in your Contacts list. You have to learn to think the way the Treo wants you to for this task, but it's not so bad once you get used to it.

1. Enter the first letter of the contact's *first* name.
2. Enter the first letter of the contact's *last* name.
3. Continue entering letters from the contact's *last* name until you have located the contact.

There is one caveat to this—if you store a contact name in the Company field of the contact record, instead of using the First and Last Name fields, Steps 1-3 will *not* work. To find a company, you simply enter the letters of the Company field in sequence.

One annoying aspect of the Treo Phone application is evident when you need to enter numbers after placing a call. For example, if you call your friend's work number and you need to enter characters of her last name into the phone system to get her extension, you are in for a surprise. Where have the number buttons, with the letters on them, gone? Indeed, they have disappeared, and you need to tap on the Keypad button to get them back, as shown in the following figure.

During a call, you can also hit the Return key to switch to the Keypad view. Push the Phone button on the Treo keyboard (called the *hard* Phone button) to return back to the normal Active Call view.

One last piece of advice for the call view—if you need to mute your voice from your caller, tap on the button with the microphone on it and this will turn off the phone's microphone. Tap it once more to turn the microphone back on.

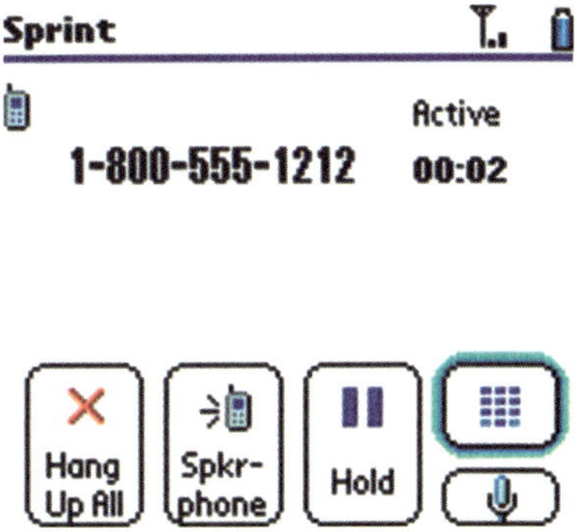


Hey, where did my keypad go?! Push the 'Keypad' button (shown with the focus ring active) to switch to the Keypad view while on a call.

In Keypad view, you are able to see the letters that correspond to the numbers. To get back to your normal Active Call view, push the hard Phone button.

## Favorites

To set up speed dial and the like, you must first understand Treo Favorites. You'd think that Microsoft would have copyrighted the phrase 'Favorites' long ago, but alas, from the Phone app, pushing up on the 5-way navigation pad gets you to Favorites.

Now there are a few things that can qualify as a Treo Favorite:

- Dialing a phone number (Speed Dial)
- Visiting a web site (Web Link)
- Launching a Treo application, like Calculator or Camera (Application)
- Sending a text message to someone (Message)

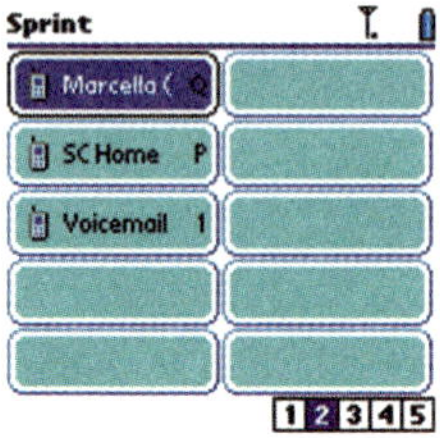


The Favorites view lets you assign hotkeys. Voicemail is a great example—by pushing and holding the 1 key from the Phone app, my voicemail is dialed.

From the Favorites screen, you can create a new Favorite activity as follows:

1. Maneuver to the Favorite button you wish to create (or replace) with your Favorite.
2. Press the Menu button, or just tap the title bar to bring up the menu.
3. Select Edit→Edit Favorites Button.
4. Select the type of Favorite activity you'd like to program. See the previous bullet list to determine what to use here. For the purposes of this example, select Speed Dial.
5. You can either perform a Lookup to populate the Label and Number, or simply enter these two fields manually.
6. Optionally, enter a Quick Key. This is where Speed Dial comes into play.

I suggest using buttons that are on the corner of the keypad for important Speed Dial Quick Keys. Q and P are useful in this regard. If you would like to use a numeric button, you are forced to enter the letter that corresponds to the number on the Treo's keypad. In other words, enter "E" for 1, "R" for 2, and so on.

There are quite a few things you can do with Favorites by tapping the More button in the Edit Favorites screen. Most useful here is how to automatically dial an extension, or other extra digits, as part of a Favorites button's action. Anything you enter in the Extra Digits field in the More Options screen will be dialed exactly two seconds after the contact's number has been dialed. If you need to work with timing, enter a comma, which equates to a one-second pause during the dialing of Extra Digits.

In the More Options screen, you are also able to select a ring tone to use when a call is received from the phone number associated with this Favorite, and you can even select an image that you've taken with your Treo's camera that appears when their call is ringing on your phone!

---

When you have a contact selected in the Favorites screen, press the space bar to get a list of all the numbers you have for that contact. You can scroll the list and dial a number by pressing Center.

---

## Skin your Dial Pad

If you get sick of looking at the same old boring blue number pad in the Phone application, it's easy enough to change them. You can also change the splash screen that shows up when you toggle Wireless Mode. Download a shareware application called Skinner, available from *http://www.79bmedia.com/skinner/*, to easily spice up the Phone application. Placing calls has never been so much fun!

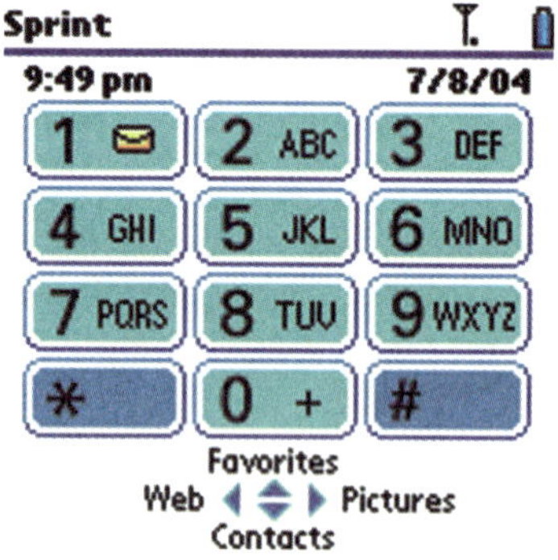


Go from the default Treo dial pad (yawn)...

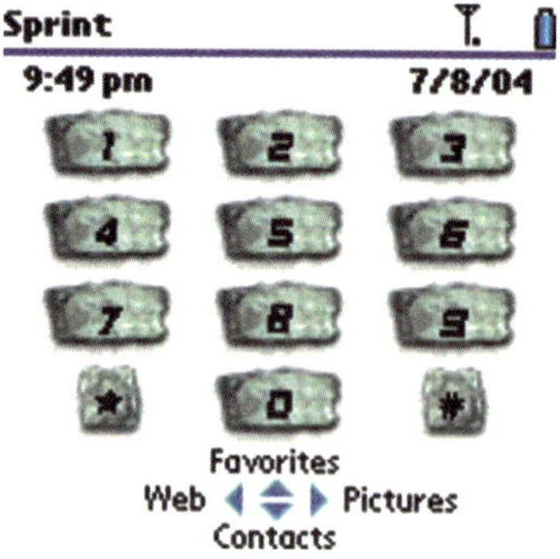


... to Fred Flintstone's dial pad! (or perhaps Bam Bam's?)

## "Sorry, my face hung up my phone!"

If you think about it, the touch screen on your Treo would be difficult to live without. With no touch screen, the only way you could tap a button, tick a checkbox, or scroll through a list would be with the hard buttons that you've probably used on a normal cell phone. Sure, hard buttons work, but the Treo isn't a normal cell phone! The touch screen is great, making it easy to drag to selected text, and allowing you to tap on any item in a long list, rather than forcing you to scroll down to it before you can select it.

However, there is a fatal flaw to having a touch screen on a smartphone. It may sound funny until it's happened to you, but it is quite possible for your face to hit the Hang Up button, while talking on a call. Oops! And if you are like me and you usually carry your Treo 600 in your pocket, you will notice a related problem. When the phone starts ringing, just *try* to fish it out without tapping on the screen and answering the call before the thing's even half way out of your pocket. The same is true for Treos that live in a purse or backpack . . . your caller will hear you fumbling around with the phone, and worse, you won't have a chance to look at the caller ID to decide whether to take the call, because you've inadvertently answered it.

There is a simple solution to this problem, but it's hard to get to, so you'll probably want to dog-ear this page. There is a Palm OS preference to disable the touch screen when an incoming call is ringing on the device. There is also a separate preference to decide if you want to disable the touch screen after you've accepted and are presently *on* a call. Here's how you can get to these preferences:

1. Switch to the Palm Launcher by pressing the Home key.
2. Make sure your Launcher drop-down list at the top left of the screen, is set to All or System, otherwise the Preferences application will be filtered out.
3. Select Prefs.
4. In the Preferences drop-down list at the top left of the screen, select Keyguard.
5. Toggle the two checkboxes at the bottom of the screen.

The Keyguard preference panel lets you control when the touch screen is disabled. I suggest disabling the touch screen when incoming calls are received.

While we're here, let's talk about the Keyguard feature. When you turn your device off (or it shuts off automatically due to inactivity), and you want to turn it on again, you will see the Keyguard message Ⓐ.

Ⓐ Love it or hate it, Keyguard comes in handy on occasion.

On the Keyguard preferences screen, you have some choices to how Keyguard is set up on your Treo.

## Disabled

Keyguard never comes up. Careful that your keys don't accidentally place a 3-hour call to your friend's answering machine . . . in Brazil!

## When power is turned off

As soon as you turn the power off (or your Treo goes to sleep due to inactivity), the Keyguard will be waiting for you when you fire it up again.

## 5 or 30 seconds after power off

After turning the device off (or having it fall asleep out of sheer boredom), you will have a 5- (or 30-) second window during which time you can turn the power back on without seeing the Keyguard window pop up.

# Extreme Calling: Juggling Multiple Calls

I don't know about you, but I am utterly incapable of handling multiple calls on normal phones—office phones, regular cell phones, home phones—you name it, I invariably lose both callers when I try to get fancy. On these phones, I just let my second caller go to voice mail, and then quickly call them back—agreeably this is a little old-fashioned, but it's a system that works for me 100% of the time. The large display on my Treo smartphone makes it a *lot* easier to work with multiple callers, such that I actually have no problems juggling the calls. In this section, I'll show you all the techniques you need, some of which are curiously omitted from the Treo's manual, for juggling calls like a pro.

## Call-Waiting

This is the most common multiple call scenario: you're talking on the phone, and suddenly you hear a tone that indicates that a second call has come in. When you look at your Treo, you will see the Call Waiting screen, which gives you the option to take the call from Caller #2 (which places Caller #1 on hold) or to send Caller #2 straight to your voice mail.

Hello, Vienna calling!

If you decide to take the second call, the call view will now incorporate both calls. The original caller is indicated as being on hold, and their phone icon becomes grayed out. This caller can no longer hear you, and thus is quite literally call-waiting. The caller with whom you're now speaking is indicated by a blue phone icon. At this state, Ⓐ your Treo can do a few things:

### Hang Up All

As the name implies, this button simply hangs up on everybody, immediately.

### Speakerphone

This places the phone into speakerphone mode. The microphone sensitivity is turned up in speakerphone mode, so you don't need to yell!

### Swap

This will swap between the caller on hold, and the one with whom you're speaking.

### Conference

Available only on the GSM Treos Ⓑ, you are able to pull both of your callers into a three-way conference call.

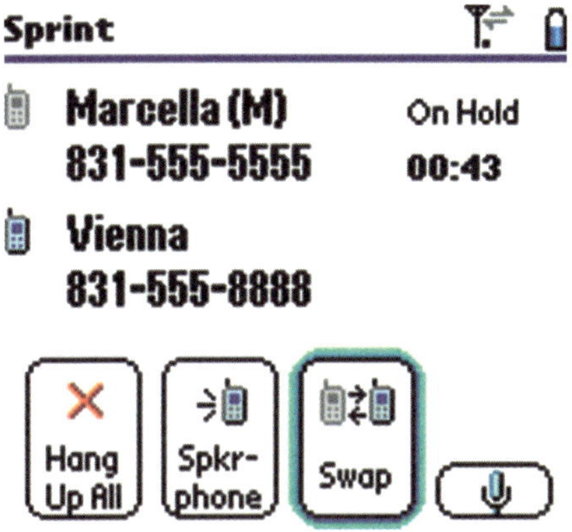


Ⓐ Marcella is on hold, and now I'm talking to Vienna. I can swap who's on hold, and who I'm talking to, with the Swap button. Because my carrier is Sprint (CDMA wireless technology), I do not have an option to engage my callers in a conference.

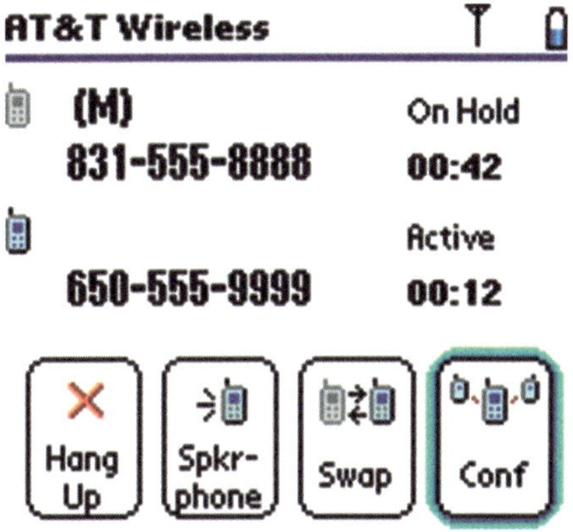


Ⓑ This Treo, with AT&T's GSM service, offers a Conf button to conference in both my callers. Also, notice that the Hang Up *All* button is replaced by a Hang Up button on GSM phones, providing a very easy way to hang up just the active caller.

If you're wondering how to disconnect a single caller on CDMA-based Treos (e.g., Sprint and Verizon), you're not alone. This is one of the most curious aspects of CDMA Treo call handling. 'Hang Up All' certainly won't do what you want! Here is a technique, admittedly convoluted, and one which some claim isn't always reliable, for hanging up on just one of your two callers.

1. Swap to the caller you wish to keep on the line, and tell her to hold on for about ten seconds.
2. Use the Swap button so that you're speaking with the caller you wish to disconnect, and give them your farewell.
3. Push the Backspace key on the keyboard. Your Treo will act as if you hung up on *both* calls, and you will likely stare at the dial pad screen in astonishment.
4. In about ten seconds, you will appear to receive an incoming call from the caller who you wanted to keep on the line. Answer the call!
5. You are now connected to just the caller you wanted to keep on the line; that caller never experienced a disconnect, only a long period of silence.

File that one under Treo Wizardry, and hope you never have to use it!

---

Only on Sprint and Verizon Treos: if one of your callers in a call-waiting scenario hangs up, instead of *you hanging them up* with the technique listed above, they will remain listed as an active call. If you swap over to that call later, you will usually hear a dial tone, and you are likely being charged for this airtime. So it's always a good idea to use Backspace to completely disconnect a caller from a call-waiting scenario. This is a limitation of the network, and not the phone: the GSM-based Treos (AT&T Wireless, T-Mobile, Cingular) work flawlessly in this regard.

---

# Conference Calls

You can have up to three callers in a conference call if you have a CDMA Treo (Sprint and Verizon); however, the GSM Treo (Cingular, T-Mobile, and AT&T Wireless) allows you to have up to six callers in a conference call. This disparity in the number of participants in a conference call is due to a fundamental difference between the CDMA and GSM cellular networks. Sometimes your service provider makes conference calling an optional feature of your service plan, so it might not be available to you. And if it is available, you can bet you're probably paying at least double airtime for the duration of the conference!

1. Dial your first attendee normally. Tell him to hold on, and press the Hold button.
2. Select the Add Call button, and your Treo will indicate that you have a call in progress.
3. Dial the second attendee. You can go to Favorites, enter the number directly, or go to Contacts to do this.
4. Once you're connected with your second attendee, press the Conf button.
5. You are now in a conference call.

It seems much easier to work with conference calls than with call waiting!

## Using Applications During a Call

For most calls, you will be chatting away while your Treo is in the Phone application, showing with whom you're talking, and for how long. If you should need to look up a phone number, or your caller requests you change the date of an appointment, or you really need to be playing Bejeweled, go right ahead. The Treo will keep your call in progress, so you can continue talking as you switch out of the Phone application and into any other application you like.

You could just put your call on Speakerphone mode, so that you're able to see your device and carry on your conversation at the same time. The problem with this is, because the microphone is on the bottom of the Treo, your callers will hear your fingers fumbling with the keys, as well as any sounds the application(s) you launch are making! One solution is to tap on the Mute button as you fumble. Another is to use one of the dozens of headsets on the market (most Treos come with one). Because the headset has its own microphone, your caller won't hear any keyboard noise, and as long as you don't have the sound turned all the way up on Bejeweled, they will be none the wiser to your gaming. I cover a really nice aftermarket headset in Chapter 6.

---

You can run most any application while you're on a call, including HotSync. However, you are not able to use your carrier's (optional) wireless Internet service while on a call. So you can't send or fetch new email, browse the web, or message your friends. You will have to hang up before you can do this.

---

## Summary

At this point, you have learned how to handle calls like a pro. You might need to revisit this chapter a few times, as it always takes a little practice to get call-waiting and conference calling dedicated to memory (in particular on the Sprint and Verizon models, where call-waiting is a little quirky). You should be starting to realize how powerful the Treo is as a phone—next up, you'll learn how powerful it is as an organizer.

# 3

# Staying Organized with Your Treo

# The Native Applications

Your Treo comes with the essential productivity applications for managing your contacts, your time, your tasks, and your notes. These applications have been shipping on Palm OS devices since the very beginning, in 1996, and only very subtle things have changed about them. The fact that its fundamental applications have changed *so little* over eight years is very telling of both the purity and the simplicity of this operating system. Today, these applications aren't so bloated with features that they practically collapse under their own weight, and *that* is a lesson for any aspiring software developer. I've said it before, and I'll probably say it again: the simplicity of the Palm OS enforces very usable and intuitive applications.

A *native* application is one that is stored in the Treo's ROM, or read-only memory, such as Contacts, Calendar, To Do List, and Memo Pad. ROM is geekspeak for "it will stick around even if you use up all your battery juice." Your Treo can lose its battery juice and lay dormant for eons. After you charge it up again and turn it on, everything in ROM will still be there!

On the other hand, these native applications do not store their data, which would be your contacts, appointments, tasks, and notes, in ROM. It's Read-Only Memory, which means you can't save any new information in it! Instead, all data goes into a second storage area called RAM, which is flexible enough to be read from *and* written to. The tradeoff for writability is volatility—in other words, if your Treo loses all of its battery juice, everything in RAM will vanish and never come back. Ever! The good news is that you can always restore your data from the most recent HotSync in the event that your battery dies. So you should HotSync daily! I'll talk about HotSyncing later in this chapter, under the section "Synchronizing to Your Desktop Computer."

Going into every single detail of these applications is beyond the scope of this book. And honestly, you'll learn more if you poke around in the menus and help screens of an application you want to learn.

When it is available to you, I suggest using your desktop or laptop computer to enter or modify contacts, calendar entries, tasks, and memos. You can certainly do this on your Treo, but it's a lot faster to make changes on your computer, and then simply HotSync them over to your Treo.

## Contacts

To get to your Contacts, you must first be in the Phone application. You can get here by pressing the Phone button on your Treo, and then pushing down on the navigation pad. This may seem a little cumbersome, but most people tend to keep the Treo in the Phone application at all times. In this context, simply pressing down isn't so bad!

The Treo is the only palmOne device that does not have a Contacts button to take you directly to contacts.

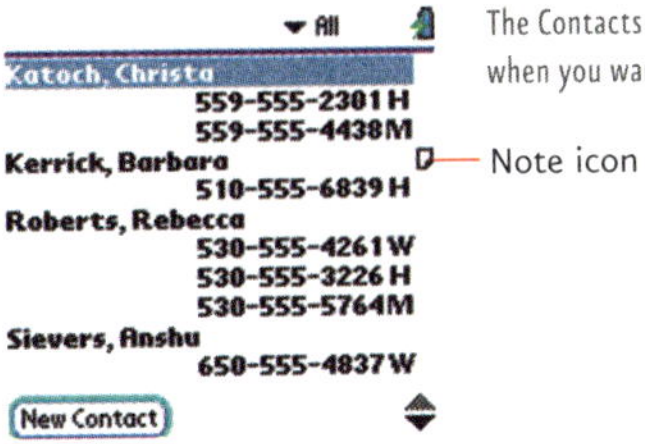


The Contacts main screen. Most often, you'll come to this screen from the Phone application when you want to dial a contact that isn't already in your Favorites list.

Here are the most common things you'll do from the Contacts screen:

- Drill down to a specific contact by typing in letters from the name. Remember, for an individual, you always want to enter the first letter of the first name, and then begin entering letters from the last name; but for a company, just start keying in the name.
- Dial a selected contact by hitting Center Ⓐ.
- Send a text message to a contact's mobile phone by selecting it. A Message button shows up for this purpose when you've selected a mobile number.

Ⓐ

- Filter the contacts by category by tapping on the All drop-down menu at the top of the screen. When you enter a new contact, you can specify the category (or make and assign your own categories) to which a contact belongs. Unfortunately, a contact cannot belong to multiple categories in this version of Palm OS.
- See all of a contact's information, perhaps to modify it, by tapping on that contact's name row.
- See the notes you've entered for a contact by tapping on the 'Note' icon.
- Create a new contact.

Many people who have used other palmOne devices are surprised when they discover the Treo does not have a button to launch the Contacts application, because all other palmOne devices have a specific button dedicated to this task. Even more surprising is that the Treo doesn't show the Contacts as an application in the Palm Launcher! PalmOne has made Contacts a component of the Phone application in the Treo, and though it may take some getting used to for users of other palmOne devices, it makes sense: Designed primarily as a smartphone, the Treo is usually going to be running the Phone application. From that context, getting to your Contacts is just a matter of pushing the navigation pad down.

## Calendar

The Calendar application, as you would expect, helps you keep track of the events in your life. Though it has the most features of any built-in Palm application, it has a gradual learning curve that allows the application to be very approachable. I've found that people have varying degrees of reliance on Calendar: some people just enter the really important events so they don't forget them, such as birthdays and airline flights; others use it to the fullest, and micromanage their workday down to 15 minute blocks. In addressing the whole range of potential users, you may find that the Calendar application has some features that you will never use. Conversely, you may find yourself wishing for things it *could* do, in which case there are plenty of comprehensive third-party Calendar replacements that suit your needs. I cover these in Chapter 6.

In my day-to-day usage of Calendar, I must confess that I barely scratch the surface of its functionality. I'm one of those people who just uses it to keep from showing up late to the really important things, like my wedding.

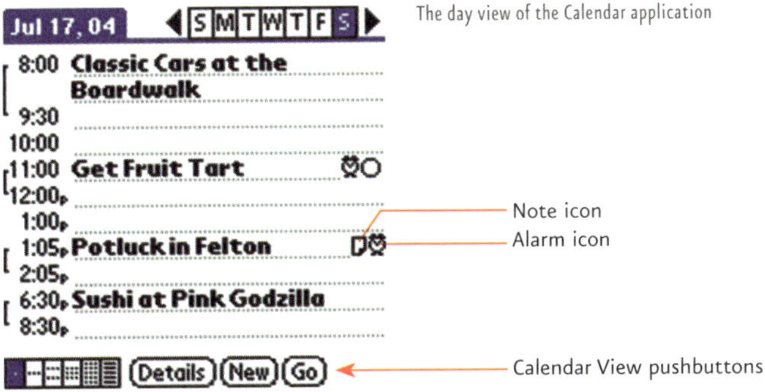


The day view of the Calendar application

The default view in Calendar is the day view, which has a list of the events for that day. If a particular event has a note associated with it, or a reminder alarm is set to go off some time before the event, you will see a note and/or alarm icon to the right of the event. The day view is compressed by default, which means that uneventful time slots are omitted to maximize the use of screen space. For example, in the day view shown in the preceding figure, the times between 3:00 P.M. and 6:30 P.M. are omitted so that I'm able to see my evening appointment without having to scroll between pages.

---

Because there are so many user interface elements in Calendar, often it's easier to use a stylus (I use my pinky finger) instead of the navigation pad to select something.

---

Here are the most common things you'll do from this screen:

- To create a new event on the current day, just type the first digit of the start time (remember to press Option to get to the numbers of the keypad), or tap or scroll down to the desired timeslot line and just type the event title in.
- To change an event's start/end times, tap on either its start or end time.
- To create or delete an event, or to modify its details such as its time range, alarm, or notes, tap the Details button.
- Use the Calendar button to toggle between the following views of your events: day, week, two weeks, month, year, and list. Or, use the pushbutton control on the bottom left of the screen to do this.
- See what's going on the previous or next day by pushing the navigation pad left or right accordingly; hold down Option to jump by week.

Option button

Details button

Calendar button

Pushbutton control

Navigation pad

Unlike Microsoft Outlook and Mac OS X iCal, the Calendar application doesn't support the notion of a single event that spans multiple days. To create such an event, specify that it repeats every day, and give it an end date.

Though the Palm OS Calendar application doesn't support events that span multiple days, your desktop calendar application may; when you synchronize such multiple-day events, they are automatically broken down (by HotSync) into duplicate single-day events on your Treo.

There are a few different kinds of events that the Treo Calendar lets you create. When you hit (New), you will have a few options.

Here's what they mean:

### Appointment

This is a normal event, timed or untimed, that can optionally have notes, and/or an alarm.

### Floating Event

This is an event, timed or untimed, that has a circular button that functions like a checkbox. "Get Fruit Tart" is an example of this.

If a floating event has not been checked off on the time (or day, if untimed) originally specified, then at midnight it will "float" over to the next day. This process will repeat until you check it off.

### To Do

This is a shortcut for going into the To Do application, and entering a To Do item with a due date. Whenever you create a To Do item with a due date, it will show up in your To Do list as well as on your calendar, and you can check it off from either perspective.

### Daily Journal

This creates a time-stamped journal entry.

### Template

If you have an event that you find yourself entering frequently, save it as a template. This lets you set up a name, alarm, reoccurrence, note, and so forth. When you want to make an actual event from the template, select a timeslot, create a new template by hitting (New), and then select your template from the template list.

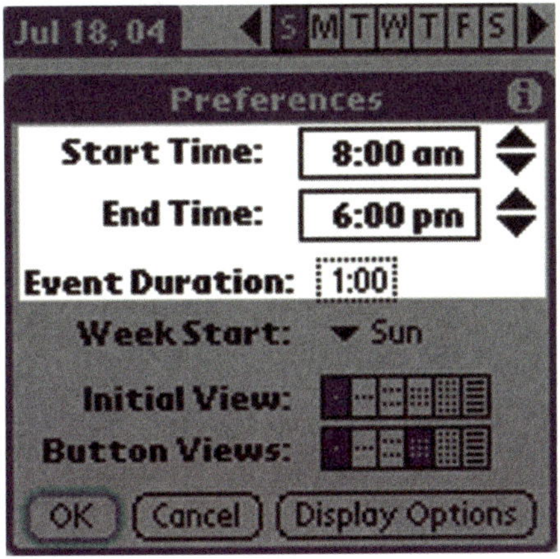


You can get to the Calendar preferences by hitting the Menu key while you're in the Calendar application, going to the Options menu, and selecting Preferences. You probably want to adjust the start and end times of your day to your liking, as well as the default event duration.

## To Do List

The To Do list is a simple application that lets you keep categorical lists of tasks, prioritize them, and check them off when you're done. You can also set a due date for any task, which causes it to show up in your Calendar view, and it will float to subsequent days just as a floating event will until you check it off.

---

A To Do entry with a due date shows up both in your To Do list and your Calendar, and will float to subsequent days until you check it off. A floating event you enter in the Calendar is very similar: while absent from the To Do list, it also floats to subsequent days until you check it off! Just remember this: if you want to be able to set an alarm reminder, use a floating event in Calendar rather than a To Do item.

---

Here's what you're likely to do from this screen:

- Check off a task by navigating to its checkbox and pressing  Center or just tap the checkbox with your pinky!
- Enter a new task. As a shortcut, just hit Center twice.

- Filter your view by toggling the Categories drop-down list on the top-right. ▾ Shopping
- Read a task's note by tapping on its Note icon.

To Do List's preferences are so frequented that they get their own button. Hit (Show...) to bring up the To Do Preferences screen.

- If you want items to disappear when you've checked them off, disable Show Completed Items in Preferences. You can always enable this if you need to see your completed items again.
- Select an item's priority to change it (make sure Show Priorities is enabled in Preferences).
- Select an item's due date to change it (make sure Show Due Dates is enabled in Preferences).
- If you need to recategorize many items, first go to the All category, and then, make sure Show Categories is enabled in To Do List's preferences. You can then tap on the category name of each item to change it.

## Memos

Memo is such a simple application that I only have one tip for you!

The Memo list

Just start typing to create a new memo.

As a shortcut to create a new memo, from the Memo list, simply start typing. A new memo will be created for you. The title of the Memo is derived from the first line of text that you enter.

# Synchronizing to Your Desktop Computer

Before I had my Treo, I had a regular cell phone that came for free with my cellular service plan. It was a decent phone, but I immensely disliked having two address books that I used frequently: one on my phone, and one in Outlook on my desktop computer. Whenever I wanted to enter a new contact, I would have to enter it in both places. If I were out to dinner with a friend and he informed me that he had a new home phone number, I would make the change in my cell phone, but would invariably forget to update it on my computer when I got home. The result was messy, and I could never really trust my address books. One of the reasons why I had no problem investing a few hundred dollars in my Treo was because it solved all of these problems through HotSync.

## HotSync and Palm Desktop: The Big Picture

HotSync is a synchronization process that takes place between a Palm OS device and a desktop computer that is running Windows, Mac OS, or Linux/Unix. While HotSync is a native application on the Treo device, you must install HotSync to your desktop or laptop computer before it can synchronize with your Treo. For Windows and Mac OS users, HotSync installs automatically as part of the Palm Desktop installer CD that comes with your Treo, although I suggest downloading the latest version of Palm Desktop from the palmOne software section of ***http://www.palmone.com***. Doing this ensures you have the latest version of HotSync, which keeps things running smoothly. There is no Palm Desktop for Linux and Unix users, but as you might expect, there are synchronization solutions, such as J-Pilot, available from ***http://www.jpilot.org***.

Palm Desktop is a palmOne application that provides an interface on Windows or Mac OS desktops and laptops for working with contacts, calendar events, memos, and to do items; it also installs HotSync, so that you can synchronize this information between your desktop and your Treo. Aside from configuring communications settings and the like, you won't spend much time (if any at all) using the actual HotSync application on your Treo and your desktop. The Palm Desktop application is where most of the action takes place because generally, it is much easier to work with this data on your desktop where you have a full-sized keyboard, a large screen, and a mouse.

---

If you use Microsoft Outlook, you don't want to use Palm Desktop to work with your contact, calendar, task, and memo data. Here's why: when you ran the CD that came with your Treo, you hopefully selected "I want to use Microsoft Outlook" during the installation process. With this option, all of your contact, calendar, task, and memo data are synchronized *exclusively* between Outlook and your Treo—so Palm Desktop is out of the picture, and will show no contents if you run it. If you wish to change whether HotSync synchronizes to Outlook or to Palm Desktop (you must select one or the other, but not both), the safest way is to perform a HotSync, and then simply uninstall and reinstall the Palm Desktop software, selecting the desired setup in the installer.

---

## Do a Normal Cable Sync

Most people use the USB Sync Cable that comes in the box, to perform HotSyncs.

USB Sync Cable that comes in the box

When this cable is also plugged into the wall charger, your Treo will charge; or, you can charge your Treo directly from the wall charger. You can also purchase a serial version of this cable for older computers that don't support USB. On average, a HotSync is typically two or three times faster over a USB cable than it is over a serial cable.

Serial Sync Cable (sold separately)

Some people prefer the USB docking cradle because it holds the device at a usable angle while it charges.

While charging, the USB docking cradle holds the device at a good angle for viewing and use.

A company called Seidio makes some of the most innovative aftermarket products for the Treo. Their Sync & Charge cable will lets road warriors charge their Treo from a USB power source, such as a laptop.

Preface
Getting Familiar with Your Treo
Using the Treo as a Phone
Staying Organized with Your Treo
Using the Internet on Your Treo
Amazing Treo Extras
Other Useful Stuff

Seidio Sync & Charge cable

The stock USB cable that comes with the Treo does *not* let you charge from USB power: you have to attach it to the wall socket charger for this to happen. And of course the Seidio cable performs USB HotSyncs, as well. Their retractable version, has an ingenious space-saving retractable cord for a little more flexibility while traveling.

Seidio Retractable Sync & Charge cable

And the best thing of all, both of these cables interface with the USB adapters they offer for automobile power sources and wall sockets. Put these on your birthday wish list!

Seidio USB car adapter and USB wall adapter

## Do an Infrared Sync

The Treo has an Infrared (IR) port, as do many desktop and most laptop computers (if you don't have a built-in Infrared port, USB to Infrared adapters are available cheaply from a variety of manufacturers). To set up for an IR sync, you need to make sure your desktop HotSync has the Infrared option enabled.

In Windows, you get to your HotSync settings by right-clicking on the HotSync icon in the System Tray (next to your clock).

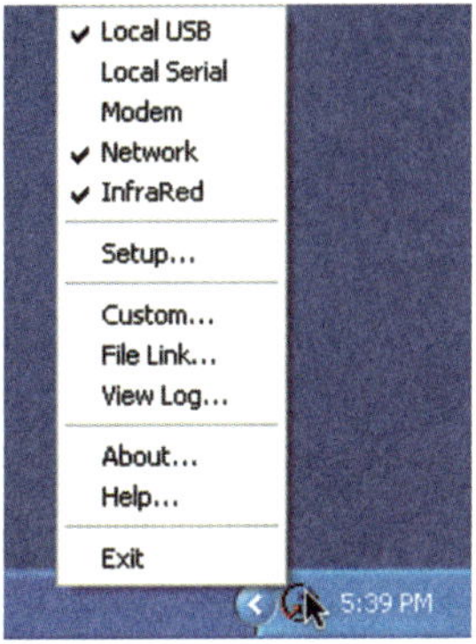


Enabling Infrared HotSync on a Windows desktop

Then from your Treo, run the HotSync application. You'll want to switch HotSync to use the 'IR to a PC/Handheld' option.

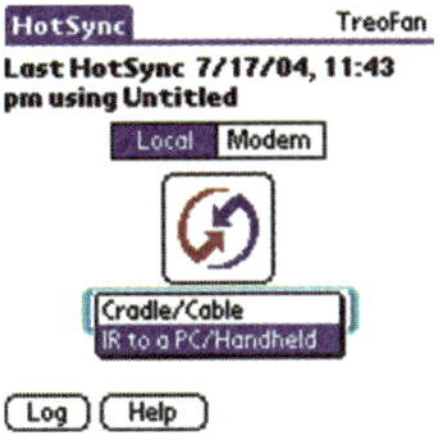


Selecting the IR HotSync option

After you've done this, it's just a matter of aiming your Treo's infrared port (located at the top of the unit) at your  desktop/laptop infrared port, and then tapping on the big HotSync button to initiate the HotSync.

## Do a Network HotSync

It is possible to HotSync to a desktop computer over the Internet. The setup can be a little daunting and, as with anything to do with networking, there are a lot of places where this might fail. If you get stuck, show this to your local network guru and she should be able to get you set up, as this is certainly not rocket science. Network HotSync is not supported on Mac OS X. The prerequisites are as follows:

- You "know a thing or two" about networking.
- You know the IP address (such as, 67.114.129.232) or the domain name (for example, ishaq.dyndns.biz) of the desktop computer to which you wish to HotSync.
- The computer to which you wish to HotSync is set up for Network HotSync, and is turned on when you intend to perform the HotSync.
- Your Treo can connect to the Internet. This is probably going to be over your cellular service provider's wireless Internet plan, though you can also use a dial-up modem on your Treo.

### Desktop setup for Network HotSync

1. Ensure HotSync is running on the desktop/laptop computer. One way to ensure this is to right-click on the HotSync icon in the System Tray near your clock, select Setup, and go to the General tab. Make sure that Always available (put in Startup folder) is selected.
2. Ensure that the HotSync running on your computer has Network synchronization enabled. To do this, right-click on the HotSync icon near your clock, and verify that Network has a check next to it.

3 Ensure your computer is designated as the Primary PC for Network HotSyncs. Do this by right-clicking on the HotSync icon near your clock, and selecting Setup. Go to the Network tab, and your HotSync user(s) will be listed. Check off those that you wish to be able to perform an Internet HotSync to this desktop.

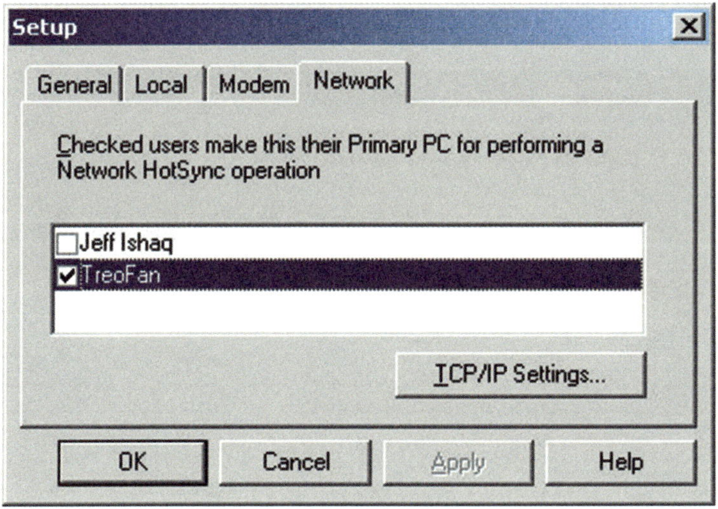


3

4. Ensure HotSync Manager is listening on your computer's TCP/IP connection. While you're in the Network tab, hit the TCP/IP Settings button, and key in the IP address of your computer. If you have a static IP address, enter this here; or, if your computer sits behind a router or firewall, you will want to enter its private IP address (for example, **192.168.1.150**). If you know it, enter your subnet mask here as well, as this will speed things up a little bit.

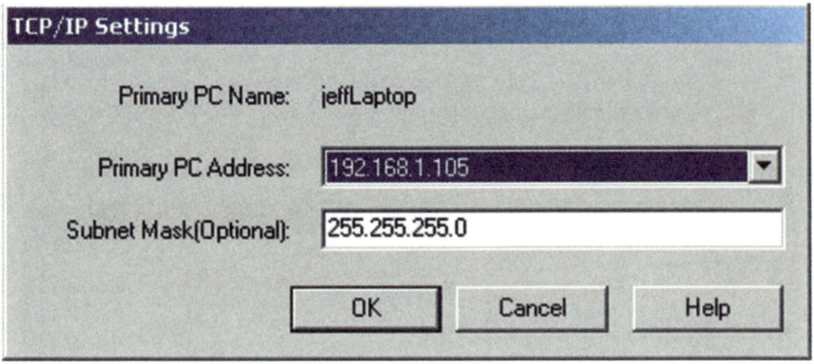


4

---

If you are unsure what your IP address and subnet mask are, you can use a utility in Windows to find out. If you are using Windows Me, 98, or 95, go to the Start menu, and select the Run option to launch **`winipconfig`**. For other flavors of Windows, you want to launch **`cmd`** instead of **`winipconfig`**. This will get you to a command prompt, where you can then type **`ipconfig`** and hit enter. You should get a list that shows your subnet mask, and IP address, as well as some other information about your network settings.

---

**Setup Network Hotsync**

5 Run the HotSync application on your Treo. Go to the Options menu and select Modem Sync Prefs, then select Network.

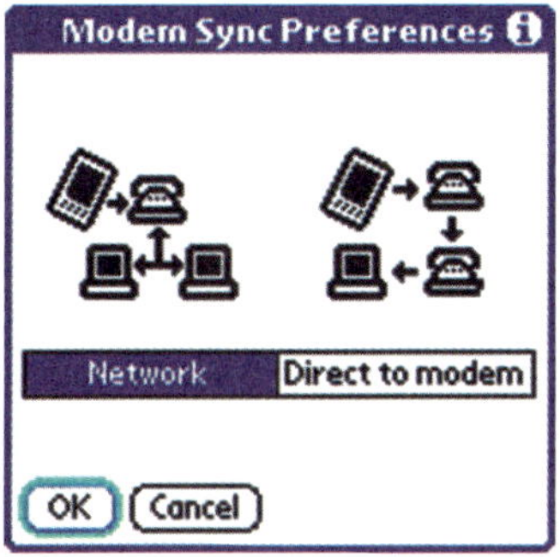

5

6 Go to the same menu and select LANSync Prefs. Select LANSync.

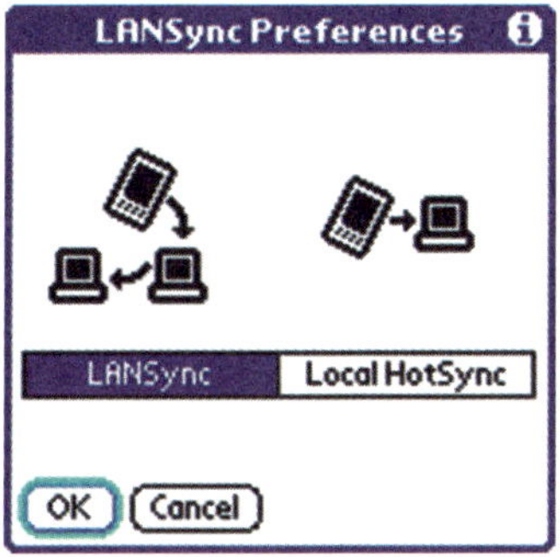

6

7. Go to the same menu and select Primary PC Setup. You can use a domain name, or a static IP address.

Domain Name

Static IP Address

## Primary PC Name

If you want to use your desktop's domain name instead of using a static IP address (do not use both), enter the domain name here. Otherwise, enter "!!" (without the quotes) to prevent HotSync from putting in the wrong name.

## Primary PC Address

If you want to use a static IP address and not a domain name (do not use both), enter it in the "Primary PC Address" field.

## Subnet Mask

You can leave this blank.

8 If you want to selectively synchronize only certain applications to save time, run the HotSync application on your Treo. Press 

, and select Conduit Setup. Here, you can select which applications will be synchronized during a Modem HotSync, which is synonymous with a Network HotSync. Changes you make here have no effect on your normal cable synchronization.

8

9 In the main HotSync screen, make sure you are set up to do a Modem sync, and that the proper service will be dialed. If you have wireless Internet through your cellular service provider, they should have set this up with you already. If you're using a dial-up modem, you simply select your dial-up Internet service provider here.

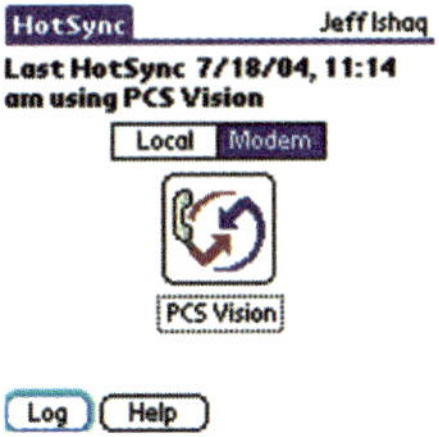


9 My Network HotSync connection setting for using Sprint PCS Vision

---

Your desktop needs to be able to communicate to the Internet over ports 14237 and 14238. If you are using a router, make sure it forwards these ports to the private IP address of the machine to which you wish to desktop-HotSync. Be warned that opening direct ports to your computer over the Internet poses a security risk.

---

## Summary

In this chapter, I've discussed little to do with the cellular capabilities of the Treo. Instead, you got a tour of the native applications of the Treo, their essentials, and tips on becoming an instant power user of them. These applications present a learning curve that is almost flat, allowing you to keep organized with a minimum of effort. The synchronization mechanism of the Treo lets you remain organized when you're not in front of your computer, providing reliable redundancy of your important personal information between your computer and your Treo. At this point, you should be comfortable using the Treo as a smartphone, and comfortable using it to work with your personal information. Next we're ready to investigate how you can use the Internet, in part to extend the access you have to your personal information to include home and work email, as well as to send instant messages between friends.

# 4

# Using the Internet on Your Treo

One of the most useful features of the Treo is its ability to get you on the Internet anywhere your service provider offers wireless data service. Once you have an Internet connection, you can use your Treo to surf to any web site you'd like, to send and receive email, and to Instant Message your buddies. You can also download audio books, and read Usenet newsgroups. That's really just the beginning—every day, cool networked applications take advantage of your Treo's data connection.

## What Is Data Service, and How Fast is It?

Your cellular service provider offers your service plan with a voice component, such as 700 minutes per month, and an optional wireless data component, which dictates what kind of Internet access you have. With the exception of some plans, using the Internet does not use up voice minutes—instead, it comes out of your wireless plan.

> Check the availability of wireless Internet service in your area, and in areas to which you frequently travel. Sometimes you can get voice coverage just fine, but no wireless Internet.
>
> For areas where wireless Internet coverage is not available, but for which you are still able to place calls, you can use a technology called CSD... if you're desperate. CSD stands for "comically slow data" ... no wait, that's Circuit Switched Data, and it essentially mimics a dial-up modem connection over your cell phone. Only, it's about as fast as a 9600 baud modem. Remember those? I had one about fifteen years ago.

The pricing and features of carriers' wireless data plans are constantly changing, and some of their representatives are woefully ignorant to wireless Internet as you and I understand it: the ability to use your Treo to surf to *any* web site, to check your email, and to tool around on the Internet without restriction to which services you can access—just as you can do from your desktop or laptop computer. So be careful with representatives who offer mere subsets of unrestricted wireless Internet access, such as a monthly service to email pictures (e.g., Sprint's Picture Mail), or a monthly service that lets you access a single email account. These are features you'd want to add to your service plan if you had a lesser cell phone that couldn't handle being connected directly to the Internet, but you've got a Treo, so insist on full Internet access. In fact, the only wireless Internet restriction you should expect to encounter from your carrier is on the number of bytes your Treo can transfer (if you don't opt for an unlimited wireless Internet plan). Here is my advice to you: before you sign up for any data plan, visit the Service Providers discussion forum on ***TreoCentral.com*** and see what the current steals and deals are for your carrier (or carrier-to-be). This is also the place to find out whether you really need *unlimited* Internet access, if (and how) you can access your corporate email with a particular carrier's plan, and so forth.

Treo's wireless Internet speed depends on your wireless service provider. The following page lists some typical rates based on reports that I've gotten. Actual performance may vary based on location and network conditions.

## Sprint

Sprint's data service, called Sprint PCS Vision, is quite fast, and tends to move about 11 Kilobytes (KB) per second. That's more than twice as fast as your normal 56 kbps dial-up modem connection.

## Verizon

Verizon's data service, called NationalAccess, uses the same technology as Sprint, and should be just as fast in the best of conditions. However, I've found that it averages about 8.4 KB per second.

## T-Mobile, AT&T Wireless, Cingular

GPRS, which is what GSM-based carriers such as Cingular, T-Mobile, or AT&T Wireless use, averages about 2.4 KB per second, and maxes out at a little over 4 KB per second. That's pretty slow, to the point that I find it frustrating to use, but in all fairness, there are still good reasons for opting for a GSM carrier. If you travel, GSM works outside of North America. Sprint won't, and Verizon won't. And GSM handles conference calling and call waiting worlds better than Sprint and Verizon's CDMA network; quite simply, GSM technology was designed better than CDMA to support these functionalities.

Alas, I'm an Internet junkie, and fast Internet access was the primary criteria for my choosing a Sprint Treo 600—I can deal with quirky call-waiting. In all fairness to the GSM carriers, some of them (Cingular and AT&T Wireless) do offer a wireless Internet technology called EDGE, which is considerably faster than anything Sprint or Verizon currently offers, but EDGE is unfortunately not currently supported on the Treo 600. Enough acronyms and tech talk! Let's move on to the primary reasons to have wireless data: web browsing and email.

# Web Browsers

Browsing the Web on a smartphone is no easy task! Smartphones aren't nearly as powerful as the latest computers, and though wireless Internet is pretty fast, it's still quite slow compared to DSL. Computer displays are capable of displaying millions more colors than your smartphone. Furthermore, most web sites have been tailored for a monitor with 800 x 600 pixels or more—your Treo has 160 x 160 or 320 x 320 pixels at best. So there's a *lot* of reformatting that has to go on behind the scenes: images have to be resized and stripped of excess colors, text and tables must be reflowed to minimize or eliminate horizontal scrolling.

This extra processing slows things down. *Proxy browsing* solves the problem by reformatting web pages on a *proxy server*, which is extremely powerful and has a very fast Internet connection. By having the proxy take care of the reformatting, your Treo gets a custom-formatted web page that looks great on the small screen.

Not all smartphone browsers use these proxy servers. Blazer, the default browser that comes on your Treo, is proxyless: it communicates directly with the web site. It's not terribly slow. But if you try out a proxy browser, you will be blown away by the speed increase! Proxy browsing isn't entirely without problems: somebody has to maintain the proxy server, which can be flooded with thousands of simultaneous web page requests, and which must be up and connected to the Internet 100% of the time. This is an expensive undertaking, so proxy browsers are rarely free. Plus, if the proxy fails, thousands of users can't use the web until it's fixed. Furthermore, because of the way some sites are, they simply don't work with proxy browsers.

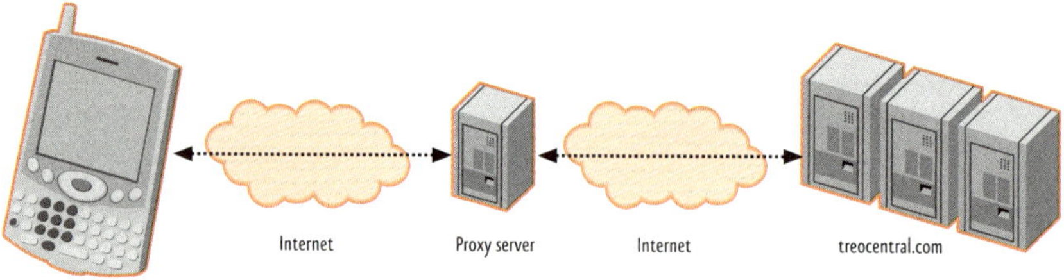


There are a few choices for browsers out there. All of them have relative strengths and weaknesses—if this doesn't matter to you, you might as well stick with Blazer, which comes with your Treo. Here are some alternatives you might want to check out:

### Palm Web Pro (proxy server or proxyless)

Some palmOne devices come with this browser, such as the Tungsten T3, but unfortunately the Treo does not. You can buy it for around $35 from palmOne's web site. Its primary strength is in downloading files, which it handles very well. It also has tons of features, as you would expect from a browser that isn't free: JavaScript, animated GIF support, offline browsing, downloading to an expansion card, and so on.

### iPanel Wireless (proxyless)

A solid browser that supports JavaScript. A free trial is available from *http://www.handango.com*.

### WebViewer (proxy)

This is a mind-bogglingly fast browser that works on the Treo. It is written in Java, and so requires that you first install a Java Virtual Machine (JVM). For more information on WebViewer, see *http://www.reqwireless.com/webviewer.html*.

### Plucker

This is a free offline browser. You set up the web site you want to download ("pluck") off of the Internet to your desktop or laptop, and then you HotSync. The web site is transferred to the Treo, and you can browse it without having any Internet connection at all.

---

Offline browsers, such as Plucker and Palm Web Pro, are handy if you are traveling somewhere where you won't have wireless data access on your Treo.

I used Plucker to download the bulk of Matt Barrett's Greece travel site, at *http://www.greecetravel.com/*, before taking a trip there. I didn't have wireless data service there, but I was still able to browse his indispensable web site offline.

---

# Email

Once you are used to getting and sending email from your Treo, you'll wonder how you ever lived without it. Sitting down at your home or office computer and checking your email is one thing, but being able to pull out your Treo while you're at Jiffy Lube and attend to all of your email can change your life forever. It doesn't matter how your email is stored, be it on an Exchange server at work, or through your Internet Service Provider's (ISP) POP or IMAP server, or even a web-based email.

## POP-based Email

POP is one the most popular ways of receiving email. If you have Internet at home, whether it is DSL, cable modem, or even dialup, you probably use your ISP's POP server to receive your incoming email. POP works very simply: when someone sends an email to you, that email ends up on the server's hard drive. When you check your email, the messages are moved to your local hard disk. Once this happens, the message has been erased from the server forever, and the only copy of the letter exists on your hard drive.

Most email programs that support POP will have an option to leave a copy of the email on the server. I suggest you enable the option to retrieve a *copy* of email messages on your Treo. If new messages come in, you can download copies of them on your Treo simply to read. When you go home and check your email on your computer, these messages will also show up in your computer's email program, where you can attend to them in full.

It's pretty easy to receive email from a POP server. When you use your Treo to *send* mail, you may run into problems. Although your ISP provides you with a server that transmits your outbound email messages, called an SMTP server, you usually must be connected to your ISP, before the SMTP server will accept transmissions from you. If you are using your Treo, you are not connected to your ISP's network—rather, you're connected to a cellular network, such as Sprint PCS Vision. So sending emails from your Treo, and using your ISP's SMTP server to send them, will result in a failure.

There are many online services that address this problem by offering a SMTP relay server. For example, ***http://www.smtp.com*** offers to give you a login and password to relay your email over their SMTP server, for $5 per month. You might also call up your ISP or cellular provider and ask them if they provide a similar service.

### palmOne, Inc: Mail

Mail comes with your Treo, and is a pretty nice mail program. It doesn't have any fancy features, but Mail does integrate very nicely with the features of the Treo, as should be expected, coming from the same company that manufactures the device itself. In particular, the five-way navigation pad is integrated very well into Mail.

PalmOne's Mail program has a robust set of auto-delivery options. This is one of its best features. Unlike other mail applications, its automatic delivery is very unobtrusive, which can be a blessing if you need to check for email frequently.

Mail has no-frills attachment support. If you have a program that is registered to handle ZIP files, such as PalmHandZipper, and a program that is registered to handle Word .DOC files, such as QuickWord, then you will have no problem opening up a zipped-up Word document attached to an email (I cover these kinds of utilities in Chapter 6). But don't expect an automated way to save the attachment to an SD card, or to beam it to somebody else. And there's no filtering at all: you've gotta pay for those kinds of features!

**SnapperFish, Ltd.: SnapperMail**

Lots of people really like SnapperMail (*http://www.snappermail.com*). It's a solid product from a great company that is well-known in the Palm community as being responsive and innovative, and it feels good to buy software from these kinds of folks. I purchased SnapperMail, and used it for a long time, but I realized one day that I don't really do any hardcore email management on my Treo, so I reverted back to Mail.

In SnapperMail, you can tap on an attachment in an email and have all the options you could ever want. This is one of its best features.

The filtering capability of SnapperMail is just a step above that of Mail: you are able to define folders and manually move email between folders. SnapperMail will cost you between $30 and $60, depending on which features you want.

**palmOne, Inc.: VersaMail**

The big strength of VersaMail (*http://www.palmone.com/us/software/palm/*) is that it can synchronize with most popular desktop email clients. When used in this fashion, you are able to carry your Outlook inbox on your Treo. If you don't have wireless Internet service, you can compose messages on your Treo, and they will be sent out over your desktop's email client the next time you perform a HotSync. If you're like me, and you keep everything important in your life in an Outlook inbox, you will find this desktop synchronization valuable. In addition to Outlook, VersaMail will let you synchronize your desktop's Outlook Express, Exchange, Lotus Notes, Domino, or Eudora email onto your Treo. While VersaMail doesn't offer a terribly flexible synchronization engine for filtering which email ends up on your device, it is a nice compromise.

If you have a bunch of subfolders in your Inbox, and thousands of email messages scattered throughout, you might consider moving to an IMAP-based email system. This makes it much easier to access all of your folders remotely, such as from your Treo.

## IMAP

IMAP, which stands for Internet Message Access Protocol, is a more sophisticated email system than POP. The physical location of the emails that you read is the primary difference between the two technologies: where POP requires you to download (move) the emails from your POP server to your local email client (whether it is on your Treo or on your computer's hard drive) before you can read them, an IMAP server holds all of your email messages on its hard drive, and you don't download individual messages to read. So when you run an IMAP email client on your Treo, and you create new mail folders, delete messages, move messages between folders, and so on, there are no messages that are being moved to your device; rather, all the work happens on the remote IMAP server's hard drive. When you read a message, or look at the list of messages in a particular folder, the IMAP server is only sending you one screenful of data at a time, more or less.

### SnapperFish, Ltd: SnapperMail 2.0 Enterprise

I covered SnapperMail already in the POP section, but the next version, SnapperMail 2.0, will support IMAP. You are presently able to download a beta version of their 2.0 product for free, which does have IMAP support. This will also let you get your corporate email from mail servers like Exchange, Notes/Domino, and Groupwise. This version will probably be an official release version by the time you're reading this. Chances are I'll be switching back to SnapperMail after their 2.0 product comes out.

### Good: GoodLink

If you're an Outlook fanatic, look no further for a corporate email solution. GoodLink (*http://www.good.com*) is literally like running Outlook on your Treo.

GoodLink's main screen is instantly recognizable to Outlook users. The column of icons on the left will whisk you off to GoodLink's email, journal, contacts, calendar, notes, and task list applications.

GoodLink has unrivaled support for viewing email attachments, allowing you to play PowerPoint presentations, read PDFs, edit Word and Excel files, and more. It keeps everything in sync over your wireless connection, so there's no need to HotSync. GoodLink is an exception to the simplicity I advocated earlier—it has features galore and a crazy user interface that spits in the face of The Zen of Palm. But if you are an Outlook fanatic, it's a worthy compromise. GoodLink is not cheap, and it requires its own server be set up inside your corporate network, so ask the boss nicely for this one.

## HTTP

HTTP email is how you get to Hotmail, Yahoo Mail, Google Mail, and so forth. HTTP really just means "over a web browser." If you think about it, HTTP email is a lot like IMAP-based email, where all your email is stored on a remote server, and reading an email doesn't mean moving it to your Treo—you just browse a page at a time. In theory, you can simply point your favorite web browser to your HTTP-based email account, log in, and go. But you will quickly discover that Hotmail and Yahoo mail's web sites are prohibitively cumbersome to navigate on your Treo's small screen. Read on for a solution to this small-screen problem.

## Treo-Optimized Web Content

Most web sites are tailored to look best in a desktop web browser. The good news is that many popular web sites offer a scaled-down version. The bad news is that most sites don't automatically detect when you're browsing from a Treo, so you must manually enter the correct URL. Here are some Treo-friendly web sites:

- TreoCentral: *http://treo.tc*
- Google: *http://google.com/palm*
- MapQuest directions: *http://www.mapquest.com/pda/directions.adp*
- Slashdot: *http://slashdot.org/palm/*
- Weather Underground: *http://mobile.wunderground.com/*
- Hotmail: *http://mobile.msn.com/hm/folder.aspx*
- Yahoo! Mail: *http://wap.oa.yahoo.com/*

Here are some portal sites that you can use to discover other Treo-friendly web sites according to your interests:

- PDA Portal: *http://pdaportal.us*
- TreoOne: *http://treo1.com*

# Instant Messaging

Text-based messaging is big business—a friend of mine informed me that in Europe, cell phones are used for instant messaging (IM) more so than for voice calls, and that European carriers can make more profit from these messages than they do from voice calls. In fact, one of the most memorable impressions from my trip to Athens, aside from the unparalleled history of the city, was the ubiquity of two things: cell phones and cigarettes. But the U.S. is catching up—text messaging and IM by phone is growing.

The Treo has a built-in application for handling the kind of text messaging that is specific to the cell phone industry: SMS, or Short Message Service (no longer than 160 characters). Originally introduced by GSM cellular providers, SMS was so popular that it quickly found global support by all cellular carriers. The SMS application for the Treo is exceptionally cool because it organizes your messages into chat threads **A**.

**A**

In addition to SMS messaging, you can use your Treo to chat with your buddies on ICQ, AOL Instant Messenger, and so forth. Unfortunately, the SMS application that comes with your Treo doesn't know how to talk to these Internet-based chat services—it *only* works with SMS messages. The solution is to install an IM chat application that can talk with these Internet chat services, and you have some choices here. The chat application with the most potential is called Chatopus (***http://www.chatopus.com/***), which runs around $15 for the registered version. Chatopus communicates over the Internet to any Jabber server. Jabber is an open protocol for instant messaging, allowing you to talk with your Jabber contacts, as well as buddies who use MSN Messenger, ICQ, AOL Instant Messenger, Yahoo! Messenger, Sametime, and others. Jabber is quickly becoming a global standard for instant messaging, so it's a safe bet.

The buddy list in Chatopus shows you the online status of all of your buddies

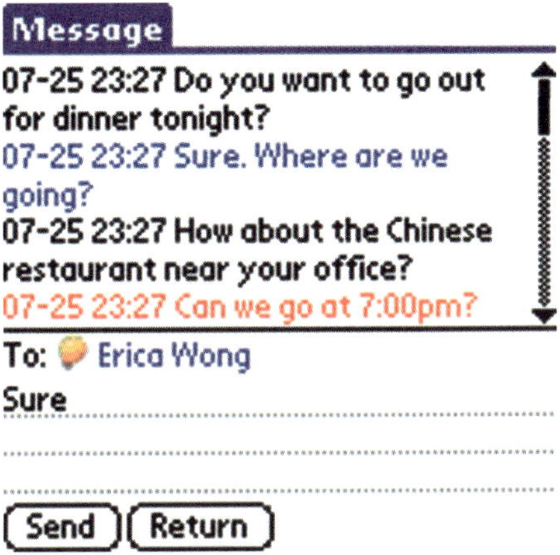


VeriChat (*http://www.verichat.com*) is another IM client that gives you a presence on Yahoo! Messenger, ICQ, MSN Messenger, and AOL Instant Messaging.

Even as you use other applications on your Treo, VeriChat will keep you on all four of these chat networks simultaneously, and also supports sending and receiving files over IM. One particularly cool feature of VeriChat is its optional ability to mask an IM as an SMS message. If you should you become disconnected from your wireless Internet service, this allows you to continue receiving your IMs. Be careful if you don't have unlimited SMS messages on your voice plan if you switch this on—it could get pricey!

VeriChat gives you a presence on ICQ, AOL IM, Yahoo! Messenger, and MSN Messenger, as the icons on the top right show.

## Summary

I've covered the basics of Internet applications for the Treo. Most of them are simply scaled-down versions of your familiar desktop arsenal of Internet tools: web browsers, email clients, and instant messaging clients. There are plenty of other Internet tools for the Treo: Virtual Private Networking (VPN) clients for connecting to your work intranet, Usenet newsgroup readers, Virtual Network Computing (VNC) clients for remotely controlling your desktop, telnet clients, and so forth. If you're looking for something in particular, perform a search on your favorite Treo software web site (see the Preface for two such sites) and you will probably have no problem finding the application you seek.

---

Because Palm OS devices have had network connectivity over dial-up modems for many years prior to the Treo devices, there is a mature set of Internet applications for them. The method you use to get a Palm OS device connected to the Internet, whether it is through an old dial-up modem, or by using your wireless Internet service, is transparent to such applications. So you can use most any Internet Palm OS application out there on your Treo!

---

Having full Internet access from your smartphone is very empowering. Once you get used to it, you'll wonder how you lived without it, especially when you travel! Next, I cover a few bonus features of the Treo that you might not have discovered yet.

# 5

# Amazing Treo Extras

At this point, you should have a good grasp of the major uses of your smartphone: working with phone calls, keeping organized (and synchronized!), and using the Internet to do pretty much everything you can do from your desktop computer. While those things should keep normal smartphone users content for a while, most people who buy Treos expect more out of their investment. As I've said, this is the best smartphone you can buy: because the Treo is such an expandable device, there's tons more cool stuff to explore out there. This chapter brings up some of the more popular extras you can use with your Treo.

# Expansion Cards for Your Treo

Most palmOne devices—including your Treo—have been shipping with an expansion card slot since March of 2001. The expansion slot, which is located on the top of the unit by the antenna, works with two kinds of media: SecureDigital (SD) cards, and MultiMediaCards (MMC).

Inserting an expansion card into the Treo: care for some Yar's Revenge?

Expansion cards come in two flavors: blank cards, and preloaded cards. You buy a blank card if you run out of memory, so that you can move some applications or data onto the card. These blank cards come in a variety of capacities. For example, you can quadruple your Treo's storage capacity with a 64 megabyte blank SD card for about $18, or you can increase the storage capacity 32 times with a 1 gigabyte blank SD card for around $140. Purchase blank cards from your local office supply store.

When you buy a blank card, make sure it's a SecureDigital (SD) card. These are more consumer-oriented than MMC cards, and are also offered in more varied capacities. On an SD card, you can toggle a tiny switch to write-protect its data, to avoid accidentally overwriting its data. MMC has no such write protection.

You will usually only see MMC cards if you buy a preloaded application. This is simply because MMC is cheaper to manufacture and to distribute.

Preloaded cards come with stuff already on them. Some of the preloaded cards that may interest you are listed below, as well as where you can purchase them:

Atari Retro (Mobile Digital Media; *http://www.gomdm.com*)
: This contains an Atari 2600 emulator, and seven games that play exactly as you remember. My favorites are *Yar's Revenge* and *Centipede.*

Mobile Backup Card (Mobile Digital Media; *http://www.gomdm.com*)
: Sure, each time you perform a HotSync, your data gets backed up onto your desktop. But if you're on the road and your Treo just lost its data because its battery got too low, you are sunk. This card will store (and restore) a snapshot of your device, and you can take it with you. A must-have for the road warrior.

Merriam-Webster Crossword Puzzles (Mobile Digital Media; *http://www.gomdm.com*)
: If *Yar's Revenge* isn't intellectual enough for you, pull from one thousand crossword puzzles and see if you can beat the clock.

*Merriam-Webster's Collegiate Dictionary* and *Franklin Thesaurus* (palmOne's Software Store; *http://www.palmone.com*)
: Ok, so I'm a nerd, but this is *my* favorite preloaded expansion card. And if I can't find the word I'm looking for here, I can always just hop over to my web browser and put it into Google. I love my Treo!

If you're using a preloaded card, simply insert it into your device, and it should automatically launch the application. If you exit the application (perhaps to take a phone call or check your calendar) you can get back to the application on your card by pressing the Home button. Then, tap the category drop-down list at the top-right of the screen. Select the card from the categories list.

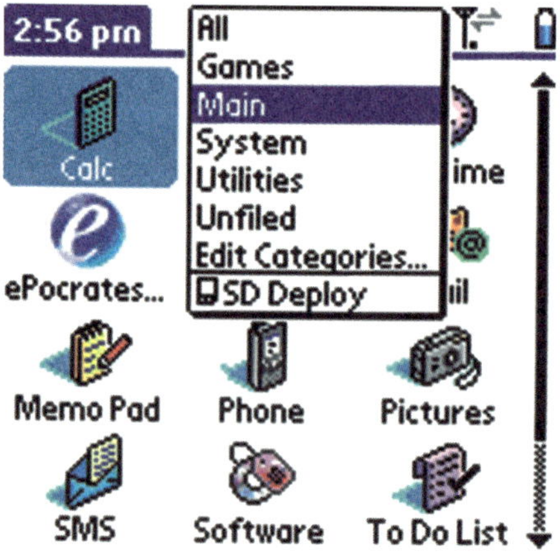


The Categories drop-down list showing an SD card. Here, I'm using a card called SD Deploy.

When you select your expansion card from this drop-down list, you will be shown any and all applications that are on the card. If the card has no applications, if perhaps it just stores your data files, this list will be empty.

You could cause irreparable damage to an expansion card if you remove it while it's being written to by the Treo. To prevent this from happening, get in the habit of always going to the Palm Launcher before you physically remove a card. You don't *have* to be in Palm Launcher before you remove a card—you can remove it whenever you'd like. However, because Palm Launcher doesn't write to the card, it eliminates the risk of damage upon removal.

## How Much Memory Do You Have?

To see how much storage space your Treo has, do the following:

1. Push the Home button to get to the Palm Launcher.
2. Push the Menu button, and choose App→Info. You should see a list of installed applications Ⓐ with a free space summary listed at the top. (I have 10.4 megabytes of free space remaining on my Treo.)
3. To see how much space is on an inserted expansion card, simply select it from the Device drop-down list Ⓑ where it will show you a listing of the applications on the expansion card, if there are any.

Ⓐ

Ⓑ

The size of an expansion card is always about 10% more than the amount of free space you actually end up with. A 16 megabyte card actually has only 14.1 megabytes of storage space that you can use.

This discrepancy is due to filesystem overhead, and to rounding, and you will notice a similar discrepancy if you look at the actual storage capacity of a computer's hard drives.

If you are beginning to run low on memory on your device, buy a large enough expansion card, and move some of your applications onto it (see "Moving Applications to the Card"). You can keep the expansion card in your Treo at all times, and the only disadvantage to running an application off of an expansion card is a longer startup time, so lots of people take this approach to effectively expand the capacity of their Treo.

An inserted SD card protrudes slightly out of the Treo case, which is an unfortunate design flaw of the device. This can cause the card to catch on things, especially when in your pocket, and might also cause the card to eject itself, fall out, and get lost forever!

Did you ever cut a notch on the left side of a single-sided 5 1/4" floppy disk to make it double-sided? If so, and if you don't mind voiding the warranty of your expansion card, you might appreciate this solution: many people report success in filing down the card with a nail file, or slicing the protruding corners off with an X-ACTO knife. In most cards, the top 1/8th inch is just plastic casing. In some cards, this will leave a split at the top, which is easily remedied by some clear epoxy and a black Sharpie pen.

A less drastic measure to prevent losing a card, and one that is also less permanent, is simply a strip of scotch tape across the inserted card.

## Moving Applications to the Card

The Palm Launcher has built-in functionality to copy an application from your Treo onto a storage card. Once an application is on a storage card, it no longer takes up space on your Treo, and you can still run it as long as the storage card is inserted in the device. Here's how to move an application, in this example FileZ, from your Treo to an inserted storage card:

1. Push the Home key  to get to the Palm Launcher.
2. Push the Menu key  and select Copy.

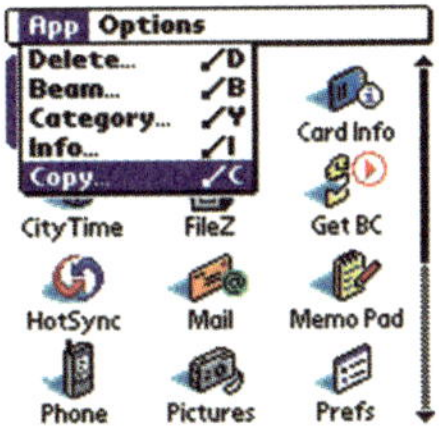


❷

3. Select the application to copy, and ensure the Copy To and From drop-down lists are correct. Then hit the Copy button.

❸

4 Copying will commence. This may take a few seconds, if the file is large.

4

5 After the copy finishes successfully, you need to delete the copy in the Treo's main memory because it's now stored on the card. Palm OS does not provide a Move option that would do this automatically. Do so by exiting from the Copy screen, and selecting Delete from the App menu.

5

6 You're done. Select the expansion card from the Palm Launcher category drop down list, and you should see your application on the card now.

6

There is an irony in all of this: because Palm OS doesn't have a Move facility, you had to approach this move in two stages: first copy the file to the storage card, and then delete the copy in the Treo's main memory. The actual file I moved, FileZ, is a fantastic file management utility that supports a single-stage move to get files to and from expansion cards, as well as numerous other extremely powerful features—and it's free. If you aren't going to be moving files around very much, stick with the steps above. But if you find yourself working with Palm OS files frequently, and you can stomach knowing what's really going on behind the scenes in a Palm OS filesystem, then FileZ is indispensable. It's covered in Chapter 6.

## Playing MP3s from Your Treo

I'm going to talk specifically about MP3 audio files for this section, but the same information applies accordingly to other sound compression schemes, such as Windows Media files, AIFF files, Ogg Vorbis, and so forth.

I finally converted my entire collection of commercial CDs into MP3 files stored on my hard drive. It took about three weeks of work, but was well worth never again having to deal with scratched CDs and temperamental CD players. As the price of blank high-capacity SD cards keeps creeping down, it becomes easier to use your Treo as an MP3 player. To be realistic, if you are used to toting 20 gigabytes of music around in an iPod, you can go ahead and skip this section. Having blown my gadget allowance on my Treo, an iPod is not in my immediate future. But I do happen to have a 256-megabyte SD card, purchased for $40, which can hold enough music to keep me content for about three hours.

Though it varies widely with the compression options used, I use the following rule of thumb to estimate MP3 storage requirements: every hour of music takes up about 75 megabytes of space. So a 256-megabyte SD card can hold about three hours of music.

If you want to use your Treo for listening to music, there are three how-tos that you need to consider:

How to get your MP3s onto your Treo
: It will take a bit of time to move 256 megabytes of files onto an SD card, but some methods are better than others for this.

How to play your MP3s
: There are some excellent Treo applications for playing MP3s, even in the background while you use other applications.

How to listen to your music
: There are cool multipurpose headsets that toggle between a phone headset and stereo headphones. And for the road, there are a few ways to feed your Treo's audio output into your car stereo.

I'll address each of these concerns in order.

## Getting MP3s onto Your Treo

There are quite a few ways of getting MP3s onto your Treo. The most common method is to store your MP3s on an SD card, which you then insert into your Treo; or, which you keep inserted into your Treo at all times.

---

> You can always store MP3s directly on your Treo's main memory, but with only around 20 MB of free space, this will fill up very quickly, and then you will have problems installing new applications, or adding new data (contacts, etc.) to existing applications.

---

So the real issue at hand is getting MP3s onto an SD card. There are two ways:

### HotSync to the card

On your desktop, navigate to the Install Tool, which is in the palmOne program group. Then simply drag your MP3 files into the main window of the Install Tool Ⓐ. Their destination will automatically be changed to SecureDigital Card. This will set the destination to your SD card's */AUDIO* directory, which is what you want. Get ready for a long HotSync though!

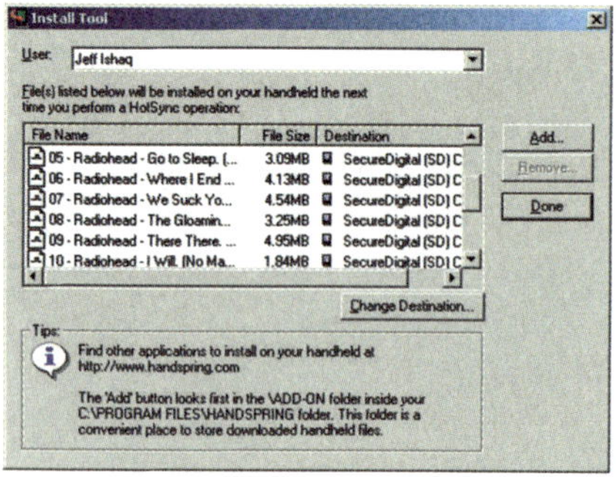

Ⓐ

After you've dismissed the Install Tool and performed a HotSync, the selected files will be transferred to your SD card. This HotSync will seem like it's dragging on for an eternity, so plan on having a slow cup of coffee while it works.

### Use a card reader

Many modern laptops, and some desktops, come with card readers that can read the same kinds of expansion cards your Treo uses (SD and MMC). Even if your computer does not, you can buy an aftermarket USB card reader for about $10 from your local office supply store. Copying the MP3 files from your hard disk to an expansion card using a card reader is always going to be much faster than using the HotSync-to-card method. When you copy files to an expansion card, there is a standard directory structure you should honor: place your files in a directory off the root level called */AUDIO.* This is where MP3 players should look to find files by default, so doing this will save some time.

If you are going to move a lot of MP3s onto SD cards, it's worth it to buy a card reader. For 75 megabytes of MP3s (about an hour of music), a HotSync-to-card will take around half an hour. A card reader will take anywhere from 30 seconds to two minutes, depending on the connection it has to your desktop (USB 2.0 or PC Card).

Keep in mind how easy it is to swap out expansion cards. If you have a couple of expansion cards, you can have different cards for different categories of music. For example, I work well to ambient music without vocals, and it's no coincidence that heavy metal gets me in the proper frame of mind for the gym.

## Playing MP3s

The Treo is very well appointed for playing music for two reasons. First, it has two separate speakers: the earpiece you use for calls, and a larger speaker on the back of the Treo. Second, the Treo uses the ARM architecture, which means it is has a separate digital signal processor (DSP) that can run independently from the central processing unit (CPU). In English, this means you can play MP3s in the background while you use other programs.

My favorite MP3 player is AeroPlayer, available from *http://www.aerodrome.us*.

AeroPlayer autodetects the MP3s in the AUDIO directory of my SD card, and isn't afraid to play them.

AeroPlayer has a two-week free trial and costs $15 to register after that time. I prefer it because it's a very simple, no-frills player, and is skinnable, with dozens of skins to choose from. It has plug-in support of audio formats, and currently offers MP3 and Ogg Vorbis plug-ins. Another popular player with considerably more features is PocketTunes.

PocketTunes (*http://www.pocket-tunes.com/*), which supports MP3, Ogg Vorbis, and WMA, also works with a streaming MP3 protocol called Shoutcast (*http://www.shoutcast.com*). After you connect to a Shoutcast server over the Internet, you can tune in to audio channels such as classical, eclectic rock, and pop rock, which are streamed to your PocketTunes over the Internet. Each channel lists a transmission speed, and as you would expect, the faster the transmission rate, the better the sound quality. If you have Sprint or Verizon, and good signal strength, you should be able to stream a 32 kbps station with no problems; otherwise, select a 24 kbps station. If you have a GSM phone, such as Cingular, T-Mobile, or AT&T, then you are out of luck: the data rate of GPRS isn't fast enough to support this kind of streaming audio. Although it has more features than AeroPlayer, Pocket Tunes has a similar 15-day free trial, and then costs $15 to register after that time.

PocketTunes is a skinnable player that supports streaming MP3 over Shoutcast.

## Listening to Your Music

The Treo has a decent speaker, but it lacks low-end response. You will need to connect it to an aftermarket headset for better sound quality. Oh, and the earbud that comes with your Treo won't work for audio: it doesn't get the output from the main speaker; rather, its output comes from the earpiece of the phone. The Treo has a proprietary sound output jack, so you will need to buy a converter for your headphones. One such converter, offered from both Seidio and palmOne for around $5, is pictured with a pair of earbuds plugged in.

Purchase palmOne's stereo headphone adapter for $5, and buy the freedom to use any aftermarket headphones you'd like.

Believe it or not, the sound output jack is a proprietary format for a good reason, and not just to force you to buy an aftermarket adapter! If you've used the mono headset that came with your Treo, you may have noticed that it has a button suspended on the wire, called the ***one-touch button***. This button functions to answer a call when the phone is ringing, and to hang up a call while talking; more importantly, it means that there's more functionality to this jack than just an audio output. Enter Seidio and their killer hands-free adapter.

Ready to rock? Seidio's 2-in1 headset has it all!

With Seidio's 2-in-1 headset, you can listen to MP3s in stereo, and it features a small in-line volume dial so you don't have to take your Treo out of your pocket to change the volume. If there's an incoming call, you will hear the phone ring in both earpieces, at which point you can answer the call by sliding a toggle to Phone mode. While on a call, use the in-line volume control to adjust the caller volume. When you are done with your call, slide the toggle back to MP3 mode, and the call is automatically disconnected. It's accessories like Seidio's 2-in-1 headset that synergize with the Treo's usability to produce a perfect smartphone, and I consider it must-have equipment.

Seidio has yet another great product if you'd like to play MP3s or streaming audio in your car. I hate to sound like a broken record here, but you've got to admit, this company really does have the market cornered on cool Treo accessories. Plug your Treo into their $40 iSound device, which sets up a local radio station in your car, and then tune your car radio to that particular station. Voila! Your car radio is now playing whatever comes out of your Treo.

Seidio's iSound lets you set up a little radio station in your car

---

If you spend a lot of time in your car, stimulate your intellect: subscribe to a service called Audible.com, which provides audio books for your Treo.

---

# Using Your Treo's Internet on Your PC

When I lived in North Lake Tahoe, the only game in town for Internet was of the 56 kbps dial-up variety. What was most frustrating was that my Treo's wireless Internet connection, for which I paid $15 per month for unlimited Sprint PCS access, was pulling in twice the speed of my dial-up modem. One morning, I had an epiphany: there had to be some way I could pipe my Treo's Internet bandwidth to my laptop. As it turns out, there is. Combined with an unlimited data plan, this can be an unbelievably useful feature for anyone who regularly needs access to the Internet: anywhere you get wireless Internet, you can share it with your laptop.

The first step to making this happen is to download a program called PdaNet from ***http://www.junefabrics.com***.

---

PdaNet is not supported on the Macintosh; however, a similar product, Wireless Modem (*http://www.notifymail.com/palm/wmodem*) is available for Mac OS X and Linux users.

---

Though the registered version of PdaNet is $34, you should take advantage of the limited free trial to make sure it works properly on your system. Installation is simple—run the PdaNet installer on your PC, select your service provider, and perform the installation HotSync when prompted. Now, whenever your Treo is connected over the USB HotSync cable (serial HotSync cables will not work), run PdaNet on your Treo and select the Connect button. You will be ready to go!

The PdaNet application on your Treo is really quite simple to figure out!

If PdaNet is able to establish a wireless Internet connection, your PC will connect to it as a virtual modem connection, and you are ready to start surfing on your PC.

Using your Treo as a wireless modem for your computer is called *tethering*. When tethering, you must keep track of how much bandwidth you use. If you pay by the kilobyte, you can rack up an astounding bill very quickly. Even if you have a so-called unlimited data plan, you aren't off the hook: some users who use a lot (one gigabyte or more per month) of data have reported receiving a nasty letter from their cellular provider, informing them that they have abused the service and may no longer use it.

If you find yourself frequently tethering to get Internet access, most providers offer unlimited data plans for laptops that are faster than what your Treo can provide. T-Mobile has the most affordable plan (but slower than Sprint or Verizon Wireless) at about $20/month, while others charge around $80/month.

I have had no problems conducting day-to-day business using PdaNet over my Sprint PCS Vision unlimited data plan. But if I were shuttling terabytes of multimedia over Sprint PCS, I could surely expect trouble!

## Summary

You've just learned about some of the coolest extras your Treo has to offer. The Treo benefits from a grassroots user base wherein a user might ask for a program or utility they've always wanted, and an enterprising developer will turn the request into a reality. I've seen this happen countless times! With the users driving the software, there's bound to be more amazing Treo extras just around the corner. In Chapter 6, I cover the essential Treo apps, as well as pointers for you to research your own Treo resources.

# 6

# Other Useful Stuff

By now, you've learned the ropes of your Treo, so this chapter isn't going to focus on any new functionality. Plus, you're probably tired of reading about all the amazing things the Treo can do! Instead, I'm going to cover troubleshooting, because you will invariably end up crashing your phone at some point. Then I'll review some essential applications. Finally, I'll cover one of the hottest topics Treo users face today: carrying cases (really!)

# Troubleshooting Your Treo

Oh boy, you've done it now. The Treo is generally a well-behaved little smartphone, but it may get fussy from time to time.

I've listed some of the most common complaints with the Treo, and solutions that should hopefully get you up and running again. These tips have been collected from my own experience, and from the forums at TreoCentral.com. If you're stuck, I highly recommend pointing your browser to TreoCentral.com and searching the forums before you bother calling your carrier.

---

TreoCentral is the de facto web site for Treo users. Developers lurk in the discussion groups and turn suggestions from group members into applications. Equipment is fairly (and sometimes brutally) reviewed, and carriers' deals, service, and speed are discussed with fervor. There is a store that has a lot of the products covered in this book, and TreoCentral has a fantastic FAQ that is growing every day.

I can't stress enough how useful a resource TreoCentral is for any Treo user. Check it out: *http://www.treocentral.com*.

---

## On Software Quality

Some of the most useful Palm OS software does not have the fit and finish of professionally-developed applications. If an application crashes your device, or is acting foolish, consider who develops the most innovative Palm OS software before you lose your temper: many are hobbyists who spend their free time learning to program so they can solve a problem no one thought of solving before.

But be patient, because this is the compromise you must make for having a thriving grassroots developer community. The flipside of the bugs and quirks is that you get developers who respond quickly to users' needs and deliver more personalized support than you'd ever get from a large software company! I think you'll agree it's a worthwhile compromise.

## My Treo has locked up!

It's not as bad as it seems—an application probably crashed and didn't recover very gracefully. Performing a soft reset (see "Resetting Your Treo") will almost always take care of the problem.

## My Treo keeps resetting!

When your Treo is resetting, it notifies every installed application that a reset has just occurred. Some applications do some processing in response to this notification, and in rare cases will crash the device, causing a second reset, which in turn causes the same application to crash again in exactly the same fashion; you wind up in an endless cycle of resets. The solution is to hold down the up direction on the navigation pad, and continue holding it down while you perform a soft reset of the device (or while it resets itself). This prevents the reset notification from going out, so the offending application doesn't have a chance to crash and reset the device anymore.

## My Treo resets when I do a Find!

This usually means an application has misbehaved when Palm OS asked it to search through its records for the keyword(s) you specified in your Find. The hard part is finding out which application it was, so that you can then email its support department.

---

After your Treo crashes, you can usually find out why. Go into your Phone application and dial ##377 for CDMA models (Sprint and Verizon), or #*377 on GSM models (all the other carriers), and push the dial button. 377 spells ERR. The system error log will display the last error that happened, if any. Sometimes it will tell you in which application the crash occurred, so you can remove it or contact its support folks for help.

---

### The Vibrate feature doesn't work anymore!

Sometimes the mechanism gets stuck. To solve this problem, put the phone on Silent Mode, assuming you have it set to vibrate in this mode, and call it from your landline. While it's ringing, hold the phone screen up, with the antenna pointing toward you. Rapidly extend your arm straight out, stop abruptly, and pull your hand back in. The idea is to un-jam the vibrator, so try to synchronize this motion with when the vibration would normally occur.

### My camera produces grainy pictures with lots of blue pixels in it!

Unfortunately, the Treo 600's camera stinks. This is why I didn't bother covering it in another chapter in this book—in case you were wondering. The poor image quality is completely normal, and you can't do anything about it.

### I can't hear MP3s out of the earbud!

The stock earbud that comes with the Treo isn't wired to get sound from the main speaker, which is where most MP3 players send it. The stock earbud only connects to the earpiece speaker, so that you can hear your caller. Your only option is to buy the stereo headphone adapter (which I cover in Chapter 5) and some stereo headphones.

# Resetting Your Treo

To perform a soft reset, take the stylus out and unscrew the tip. On the opposite side of the tip is a thin plastic rod that you can insert into the reset hole on the back of the device. A soft reset will simply reboot your phone, and will not result in any loss of data, though you may have to toggle wireless mode back on after the soft reset by holding down the power button for a few seconds.

To perform a hard reset, hold the power button down while performing a soft reset. When the device resets and you see the "Palm Powered" logo, release the power button and you will be asked if you want to erase all data. To commit the hard reset, press the up direction on the navigation pad; push any other button if you've changed your mind. They really mean it: **a hard reset will cause all of your data and all of your settings to be lost**. Sometimes you have to do a hard reset when your carrier issues a firmware upgrade. As long as you perform a HotSync immediately before the hard reset, and again immediately after, all of your data will be safely recovered.

# Essential Applications

These are applications to make your Treo even more productive and easy to use than it already is. I selected these by talking with countless other Treo users, and using my best judgment to narrow it down to just ten applications. These are essentials, so I suggest you download and install all of these sooner, rather than later. All of them offer free trials, and some of them are totally free, so you don't have anything to lose!

## Agendus

One of many views that Agendus offers of your pressing issues

Agendus is $29.95 from ***http://www.iambic.com***, and offers a free trial. This is *the* aftermarket solution to the Treo's native personal information management (PIM) applications. It has a ton of views, its display is extremely customizable, and it lets you link contacts into meetings and tasks. Because Agendus has been around forever, it shows a great level of refinement in its interface and its functionality. Agendus works with the native data from your PIM applications, which is great: you definitely want to avoid aftermarket PIM solutions that store their data in their own proprietary format, as no other applications will know how to access your PIM data!

## Bob's Alarm

Bob's Alarm Clock also has a timer and a stopwatch.

Bob's Alarm Clock is $9.50 from ***http://www.handango.com***, and it offers a free trial. It offers all the features you could ever want in an alarm clock, yet still has a very simple and aesthetically pleasing look to it. You can change the background, use WAV and MIDI files as alarms, and set multiple alarms. It comes with special alarm tones that are considerably louder than usual for those heavy sleepers among us!

## Butler

Butler lets you control all those things palmOne forgot about.

Butler, formerly TreoButler, is available on PalmGear for around $7, and has a free trial. This application has been forged over time by the input of users on the TreoCentral forum, and is a great example of how grassroots development really benefits Treo users. You can feel good about buying this. Butler grants you control over all the things on your Treo that you are astonished you can't configure. Like assigning keyboard shortcuts to your favorites and having them work anywhere, not just inside the Phone application. And making the Treo's LED flash green when a voicemail is waiting. And a bunch of other things too.

## FileZ

FileZ lists your files in any sort order you could imagine.

FileZ, available from PalmGear.com, is absolutely free. You would be hard-pressed to find somebody who doesn't put this utility on their Top 5 list of essentials. For me, it is *the* essential application, the one I install before any others. FileZ lets you do anything you could ever want with the files on your device (as well as ROM-based files), including beaming them, moving them to an expansion card, renaming them, deleting them, and tons more.

## Graffiti Anywhere

As the name implies, you can enter graffiti anywhere on the screen.

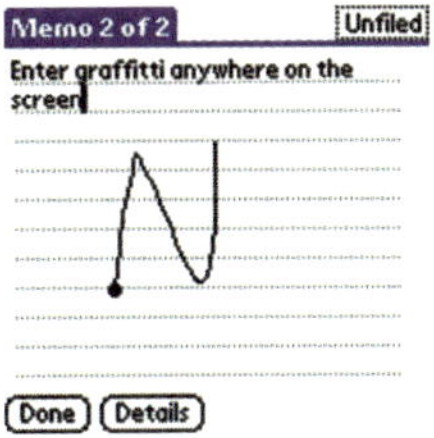


Graffiti Anywhere is available from PalmGear.com, and is absolutely free. This utility isn't for everybody, but most anyone who used Palm OS prior to getting a Treo will want this. While the keyboard is great for entering text, some people still get around on the device better with Graffiti.

## HandZipper

HandZipper's user interface is utilitarian and pragmatic: I love it!

HandZipper, from ***http://www.handwatch.com***, has a free lite version and a full-featured version for $9.99. The most common use for this utility is to open up a file you've downloaded over your wireless Internet connection; or, to open up a zipped email attachment. HandZipper will let you unzip files from an expansion card into main memory, and it has a built-in text viewer for reading zipped-up text documents. You never know when you'll run into a zip file, so install this utility sooner rather than later.

## KeyCaps600

Careful, it's really easy to get hooked on KeyCaps600.

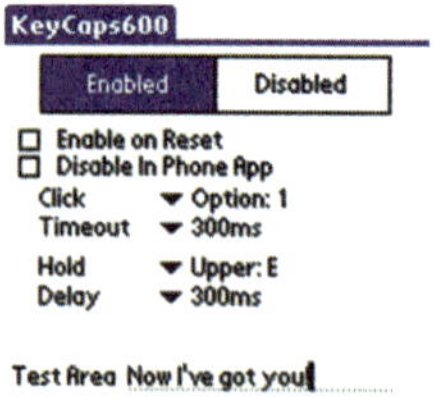


KeyCaps600 is available from PalmGear.com for $10, along with a trial version. By holding down a button for a quarter of a second, that button's capital letter will appear. And if you hit a key twice in quick succession, its option character will show up; in other words, the character you would get to by first hitting the option key. Is this worth $10? Download the trial and get a feel for it, and then see how long you can live without it!

## LightWav

LightWav lets you configure your Treo sounds using all the popular sound file formats.

LightWav is $16.95 from PalmGear.com, and a trial version is offered. It will let you replace any of your Treo's alarms and ringtones with a sound file of one of the following formats: MP3, WAV, OGG, WMA, and MIDI. The sound file can be of any length, as long as there's space on your Treo for it. I use this to have my desktop Outlook's "new mail" sound play when I get an incoming message. I'm conditioned to pay attention to this noise, while ignoring most other sounds coming out of my computer, so this works out very nicely.

## QuickOffice

QuickOffice makes it easy to read Word, Excel, and PowerPoint email attachments. Working with them isn't as much fun due to Treo's small screen.

QuickOffice, available from *http://www.handango.com*, costs $39.95 and offers a free 15-day trial. There are a few Office suite applications out there for Palm OS, and QuickOffice is my favorite for two reasons. First, they have responsive and personal customer support, so it doesn't feel like you're working with a soulless corporate entity. Second, QuickOffice supports native Office documents. While some office suites use proprietary formats for representing your Office documents, QuickOffice uses the native desktop format. This means you are able to load Office documents straight on to your device via infrared beaming, from email attachments, or from expansion cards.

I'm not much of a road warrior, so my main use for QuickOffice is for working with my gym log. I maintain my workout schedule in an Excel spreadsheet, and I have QuickOffice set up to synchronize it with my Treo. So I can update the spreadsheet at the gym, and next time I HotSync, those changes appear on my desktop version (and vice versa). I also receive lots of Office documents as email attachments when I'm away from my desk, and it's nice to be able to review them on the go.

## ZLauncher

ZLauncher takes a while to get used to, but it gives you so much power over the normal Palm Launcher that it's worth it.

ZLauncher is $12 from PalmGear.com, and offers a 30-day free trial. It has long been the best Palm Launcher replacement around. Its strength is in its customizability and the scads of themes you can download and try out. It is packed full of useful features too numerous to list, but my favorites are its hierarchical view for browsing an expansion card, and tap-and-hold. With tap-and-hold, I can tap on an icon for a split second, and a menu will pop up that gives me the options to beam the file, delete it, get information on it, and so forth. It will take you a while to get the settings configured to your liking, but once you do, it can really make your Treo look and act sharp.

# Essential Cases

The Treo has countless aftermarket cases it. I really mean this—there are so many dozens of cases that it's hard to keep track of them all. Though the Treo comes with a sleeve, most every Treo user will want to purchase a *real* case right away. You have to be careful buying cases, as some fit better (or worse) than others. I've narrowed down what seem to be most popular cases among Treo users. The best place to go for unbiased information on such accessories is none other than ***http://www.the-gadgeteer.com***, where Julie and Judie have been reviewing Palm-related goodies for many years.

## PalmOne's Treo Form Fit Case, $29.99 from www.palmOne.com

The Treo Form Fit Case, front and back. The back has a handy detachable camera flap.

This is the most popular leather Treo case. It is reasonably priced, fits like a glove, and interfaces nicely with the included beltclip, allowing the Treo to rotate freely when on your belt, and allowing you to attach and remove your Treo from your belt clip very easily. If you're looking for a more unique and stylish leather case, look no further than Vaja (***http://www.vajacases.com***), who produce the finest leather cases available, but they are not cheap!

## Innopocket Treo 600 Hard Case, $34.95 from store.treocentral.com

Innopocket's hard case is to be used when it is closed. It was carefully designed to still allow access to everything, including the camera and five-way pad. Rubber grippies, partially visible on the right of the case above and below the hinge, keep it from sliding out of your hand. You can even slip an expansion card into the case.

You can stash an expansion card inside the lid of the Innopocket hard case!

You should see my Treo. Two weeks before finishing this book, I had a mishap while mountain biking and cracked the screen (I take my Treo with me *everywhere*). The device still functioned, but the bottom third of the display was an opaque blur of blue and yellow LCD "ink"—quite pretty, actually, but this prevented me from seeing most buttons and dialog boxes, which tend to be at the bottom of the screen. I now see the value in this strange-looking case. This thing is lightweight but very strong, and very stylish. It has a rotating belt clip very similar to the Treo Form Fit Case. If you have a job (or hobby) that may subject your Treo to abuse, consider getting this case so you don't end up like me: having to pay a few hundred bucks for a repair, being without your phone for a few weeks, and worst of all, having to deal with the bureaucracy of your service provider. Once you slide your Treo in the case, you keep it *closed* while you're on a call. Talking into a metal case takes some getting used to, but take it from me, the protection it affords is worth it. You really don't want to break your screen.

## OP/TECH USA Soft Pouch, $14.50 from www.optechusa.com

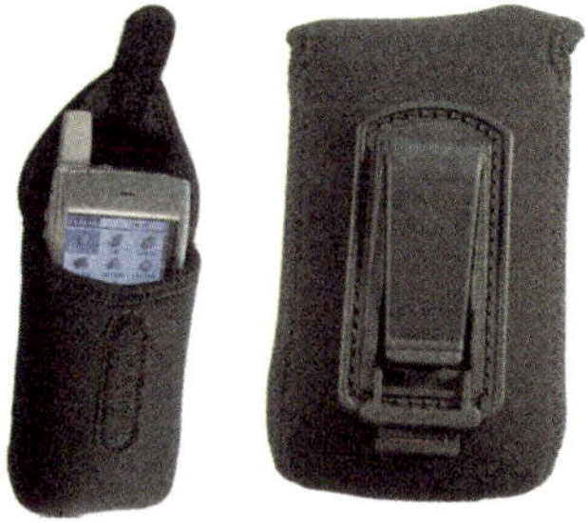

The OP/TECH soft pouch is a great softcase. It has excellent stitching, and a reasonable price. It doesn't get in the way when you sit down, and its belt clip is sturdy enough to ensure it will never unexpectedly fall off of your belt. I like this case because it's not Treo-specific, and works great for holding other things, such as other handheld computers, or my digital camera. OP/TECH has cases for everything imaginable, so be careful poking around on their web site or you might end up with more than just a Treo case.

## Summary

I hope this chapter lived up to its name. Once you were familiar with the basic functionality of the Treo, I hoped to provide a starting point for you to explore some of the more time-consuming nuances, such as troubleshooting and checking out some essential software. And this is just the beginning—once you start downloading and installing applications, and you spend an hour or so on TreoCentral.com, you will find endless cool things you can do with your Treo. I'll see you in the forums!

# Index

## R



## S



## T